Expressions

Taking Extraordinary Photos for
Your Scrapbooks and Memory Art

North Light Books
Cincinnati, Ohio
www.artistsnetwork.com

**Donna Smylie &
Allison Tyler Jones**

11 10 09 08 07   5 4 3 2 1

Distributed in Canada by Fraser Direct
100 Armstrong Avenue
Georgetown, ON, Canada L7G 5S4
Tel: (905) 877-4411

Distributed in the U.K. and Europe by David & Charles
Brunel House, Newton Abbot, Devon, TQ12 4PU, England
Tel: (+44) 1626 323200, Fax: (+44) 1626 323319
Email: postmaster@davidandcharles.co.uk

Distributed in Australia by Capricorn Link
P.O. Box 704, S. Windsor, NSW 2756 Australia
Tel: (02) 4577-3555

Library of Congress Cataloging-in-Publication Data
Smylie, Donna, 1953-
  Expressions : taking extraordinary photos for your scrapbooks and memory art / Donna Smylie and Allison Tyler Jones. -- 1st ed.
      p. cm.
  Includes index.
  ISBN-13: 978-1-58180-909-1 (pbk. : alk. paper)
  ISBN-10: 1-58180-909-3 (pbk. : alk. paper)
  1. Photography--Handbooks, manuals, etc. 2. Scrapbooks--Handbooks, manuals, etc. I. Jones, Allison Tyler, 1964- II. Title.
TR146.S5465 2006
771--dc22
                            2006024856

Editors: Darlene D'Agostino and Jessica Strawser
Designer: Lisa Kuhn, Curio Press, LLC
Production Coordinator: Greg Nock
Cover Photography: Front cover, far left, Kathryn Langford; left center, Barb Uil; far right, Kathryn Langford; back cover, top right, Barb Uil; bottom right, Kim Heffington

METRIC CONVERSION CHART		
TO CONVERT	TO	MULTIPLY BY
Inches	Centimeters	2.54
Centimeters	Inches	0.4
Feet	Centimeters	30.5
Centimeters	Feet	0.03
Yards	Meters	0.9
Meters	Yards	1.1
Sq. Inches	Sq. Centimeters	6.45
Sq. Centimeters	Sq. Inches	0.16
Sq. Feet	Sq. Meters	0.09
Sq. Meters	Sq. Feet	10.8
Sq. Yards	Sq. Meters	0.8
Sq. Meters	Sq. Yards	1.2
Pounds	Kilograms	0.45
Kilograms	Pounds	2.2
Ounces	Grams	28.3
Grams	Ounces	0.035

fw
F+W PUBLICATIONS, INC.

Dedication

We would like to dedicate this book to all budding photographers who take thousands of photos, trying to capture the events in their lives and the essence of those they love. For those photographers who want to give up in frustration, but pick themselves up and try again and again, this book is for you.

Table of Contents

Barb Uil

Barb Uil

Amanda Keeys

Barb Uil

Image Gallery (page 70)

Introduction

Your Creative Guide to Meaningful Photography

What This Book Is NOT

Before we tell you what this book is, we should probably tell you what it's not. Contrary to our codependent tendencies, this book will not be everything to everyone. You will find no photos of landscapes or hummingbirds. We are, unapologetically, people photographers.

What This Book IS

This book will focus on the creative aspects of photography that are often overlooked in traditional photo education due to an overemphasis on the technique of photography. We are all about the heart and soul of photography—we want to give you just enough technical information to allow you to achieve your vision but not so much that you get a headache.

This is the book we've always wanted to read; a workbook, of sorts, about making great photos of the people you love; about capturing everyday moments in extraordinary ways. A book that gives you the straight scoop on composition and lighting without getting bogged down in scary technical detail.

Throughout the chapters you will learn how to capture artful images of the people most important to you, images bursting with meaning and emotion and failing that, at least great lighting!

The first half of the book is dedicated to understanding the two most important elements in photography: composition and lighting. If you can internalize the lessons in these two sections, you will be a better photographer immediately. Today. Right now.

The second half of the book is a breathtaking gallery. Each gallery chapter begins with a down-to-earth strategy for creating images of a particular stage of life. Every concept is then illustrated in straightforward language, together with easy-to-understand visuals and tips designed to help you re-create the results for yourself.

We hope this book—brimming with inspirational images from a variety of talented photographers—will inspire you to bust out your camera and find your own unique photographic style.

All the best,

Donna and Allison

7

Photography Equipment
What You Need to Get Started

As you flip through the following pages you will note that we have assumed most readers will be shooting digitally. If you are a film shooter, not to worry: All the techniques are the same for film with regard to lighting, metering, etc.

What do I have to have? When dipping your toes into the waters of photography, it is sometimes tempting to take a leap into the deep end and end up in over your head before you even begin. This is why we have made checklists for the tools you will need to accomplish your goals in photography.

What kind of camera do I need? While many of the techniques explored in this book can be accomplished with a point-and-shoot camera, those who wish to explore photography as a lifelong pursuit should strongly consider purchasing a Single Lens Reflex (SLR) Camera with the following features:

- Interchangeable lenses
- Auto focus
- Both full manual settings and various automatic settings

Only you can decide what you want to do down the road, but an SLR will allow you to grow with it. Good, entry-level digital SLRs with a kit lens start at five to six hundred dollars and go up from there. Stick with the major camera brands and you can't go wrong. Donna shoots with Canon equipment and Allison uses Nikon equipment.

What is the best investment I can make? The camera is important, but the most important equipment you will ever buy are your lenses. If it comes to a choice between a less expensive camera or less expensive lenses, pick the less expensive camera and put the money into your lenses. You'll never regret it.

Is there a way to try before I buy? Save yourself the buyer's remorse and rent before you buy. In any major city there are camera stores that rent photographic equipment to their customers. Rent a digital camera and/or lens for a weekend and see if you like it before you invest.

Are there any other rules of thumb for buying equipment? The equipment doesn't make you a better photographer, your technique and vision alone can do that. So don't buy a certain lens because you think it will make your photos better. Our rule of thumb is that we only buy new equipment when we get to the point that we can't accomplish our vision with what we already have. For example, if we find that we are going to be shooting a lot of sports photography and the only lenses we have are 17-55mm lenses, we might consider investing in a telephoto zoom lens of 70-200mm to get the shots from the sidelines.

A Beginner Photographer's Checklist

- SLR camera (digital or film)
- Lens (many SLR cameras come with a 17-35mm or 18-70mm kit lens—these are a good starting point)
- Decent camera bag to secure your equipment
- Notebook for making notes, collecting ideas

If you are shooting digital:
- Digital media cards (your digital "film")
- Desktop or laptop computer
- Photoshop Elements or Adobe Creative Suite 2 Image Editing Software

What You Need to Take It to the Next Level

- Handheld incident light meter
- Reflector
- Additional lenses
- Tripod (if you must)

What You Need to Shoot in a Studio

- Studio lights (hot lights or studio strobe)
- Light modifiers (i.e. softboxes, umbrellas, etc.)
- Backdrops

Our Favorite Equipment

Donna Smylie

I shoot exclusively with Canon equipment [visit www.usa.canon.com or call (516) 328-5000 for more information]. I do all of my portraiture using 70-200mm lens, but have recently fallen in love with Canon 85mm 1.8. The lens is light and very portable. The background blur is exceptional and gives great isolation of subject, even in poorly lit situations. The downside is that your feet are the "zoom" on this lens. For a less expensive, general all-round wide use lens, I shoot with Canon 28-135mm (3.5-5.6). It has a built-in stabilizer and is a good lens for well-lit groups and portraits.

Allison Jones

I shoot exclusively with Nikon equipment [visit www.nikonusa.com or call (800) NIKONUS (800-645-6687) for more information]. I love the 70-200mm 2.8 VR zoom lens because it is very fast (good in low light) and the VR stands for Vibration Reduction, which makes for sharp photos even if I'm not using a tripod (which I am often too lazy to do). It compresses the image and is very flattering for portraiture work. It also allows me to be a "fly on the wall" and capture photos from a distance.

Kathryn Langford

9

The Five 'S's of Composition

Kathryn Langford

The goal for understanding composition is to allow you to not only compose better images while you are shooting, but to make sense out of those happy accidents and repeat them the next time around.

Composition is, simply, what you have decided to include in the frame of any given photo and the absence of what you have left out. Seems obvious, but it's really not any more complicated than that. However, deciding what to include and how to include it is the tough part.

Good composition organizes the elements of a photo in a harmonious way. It first attracts and then maintains the viewer's interest in the image. Some photographers have a natural eye for composition, but for every photographer, well-composed images combine a personal vision with the trial and error of hard work and practice. The bad news is you have to practice; the good news is that, with practice, you will improve over time.

There are five basic concepts that an accomplished photographer knows about composition:

SEE THE POSSIBILITIES 〉 *Identify images you love and begin to see the world in a compositional canvas of photographs waiting to be made.*

SUBJECT 〉 *Learn the difference between a specific image and an image with universal appeal. Learn to emphasize the subject you are photographing.*

SIMPLIFY 〉 *Practice simplifying your images by observing how line, shape and the rule of thirds influence a photograph.*

SETTING 〉 *Figure out how to exploit a setting for the best image using the location, background and any available props. Try differing viewpoints for more interesting shots.*

SHARE THE STORY 〉 *By including the symbols and emotion from everyday life, create images with lasting emotion and power.*

With camera in hand, let's explore the Five 'S's of Composition.

Amanda Keeys

11

See the Possibilities

In this media-saturated age, we are bombarded daily with thousands of images—so much so that we have actually become very sophisticated critics. We aren't satisfied with having photos of our children that look like they came from the local school photographer. Nope, we want our kids' photos to look like the GapKids ads. The problem? When we know what we want but we don't know how to get it.

Stop for a moment and pay attention to the people around you. The beauty of humanity is that we are all unique. You must learn to see and appreciate those differences before you can capture them in an image.

Kim Heffington

Identify Your Influences

The ideal way to begin your photographic journey is to immerse yourself in the work of the best photographers. The painters of the Renaissance were apprenticed to master painters to learn their craft. Only after they learned the principles of those skills were they free to explore their own style. Find your own influences in the work of photographers that you admire, then try to simulate what they have done in your own work. It won't take long before copying someone else's work evolves into finding your own style while you put your own spin on their initial ideas.

Audrey Woulard

PHOTO NOTES

Inspiration File

Collect images from magazines, books and the Internet—LOTS of images, images that speak to you on an emotional level, images that grab your attention and don't let go.

Once you've made your stack, lay the images out. Can you identify a common thread among them? This is the first step in identifying what you love, which is a great way to begin developing your own photographic style.

☆ **Subject** Is there a common subject, such as all children, families or adults? Are they shots of events in life, or just slices of life? Do you respond more to single portraits or to group shots that show relationships?

☆ **Lighting** Does there seem to be a common element in how the photographs are lit? Are they bright and sunny, or dark and moody?

☆ **Style** Do your picks demonstrate a casual feel or a more formal style? Are the images color or black and white?

☆ **Theme** Do your selections show life's big picture, or focus on a minute detail? Is there a recurring theme or message evident, such as family, hope, innocence or despair?

13

Practice

Once you have identified a style you'd like to try, it's time to put your vision into practice. Unfortunately, there is absolutely no substitute for practice. We wouldn't expect a concert violinist to pull out her instrument only for concerts, yet how often do we dust off the camera for just the big events of life instead of playing and practicing with it every day?

Limit Your Variables

While shooting to learn, it is important to limit your variables. Forget three changes of clothes and five different backgrounds. Start with one cooperative subject in one outfit and one environment and save the variation for creative composition and framing. By limiting the variables of what you are shooting, you become free to experiment with composition.

PHOTO NOTES

Change It Up

Try shooting the same subject...

- ☑ *at a wide angle and up close.*
- ☑ *with both a vertical and horizontal camera orientation.*
- ☑ *with lots of background.*
- ☑ *zoomed in tight.*
- ☑ *smack in the middle of the frame.*
- ☑ *off to one side of the frame.*
- ☑ *from a high angle looking down.*
- ☑ *from a low angle looking up.*
- ☑ *from all sorts of tilted camera angles for interesting shots.*

PHOTO NOTES
Self Evaluate

Print out your images and critique them.

- ☑ *Can you identify the compositional guidelines that you followed (or didn't follow)?*

- ☑ *Did the photo work? Why? Why Not?*

- ☑ *Ask a fellow photog, one whose skills are more advanced than your own, to give you a critique of your images. Online photo forums are a great place to get critique and support.*

Now, Redux! *Go back and shoot the same subject/setup over again and apply what you learned the first time around.*

Planned Spontaneity

Isn't that an oxymoron? Being prepared does not equal the death of spontaneity. In fact, it creates an environment in which you can successfully capture the most fleeting moments. Successful photographers know how to observe a setting and subject and then make decisions to ensure the best chance of technical success. Once they know they can get the shot, they can then be completely in the moment with the subject, a "fly on the wall," capturing moments of emotion that would escape a less practiced photographer.

Photographing the birth of a baby requires quick reflexes under less than ideal circumstances. How do you capture the miracle of birth in a sterile, badly lit, hospital environment? In the photo series shown here, the photographer used a lens (85mm Prime) ideal for working in low light and long enough so she didn't have to be intrusive with film (ISO 400) fast enough but not so fast that you get lots of grain.

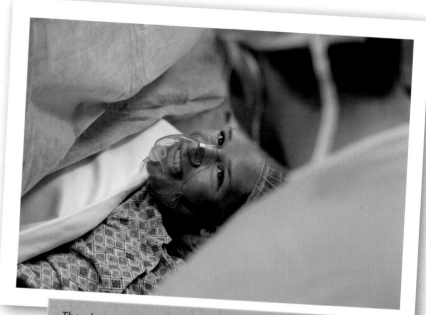

The photographer wanted to capture this couple's last minutes together before they became parents—her look of trust and love.

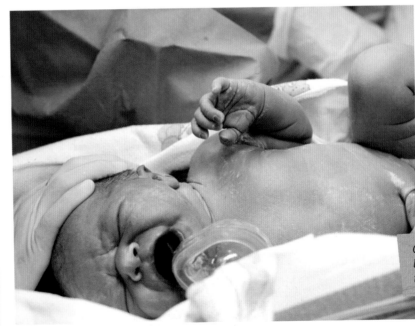

Converting the image to black and white removes the redness of a newborn.

16

An hour or two later in the hospital room, the photographer asked the father to strip off his shirt and cuddle the baby while she snapped a few shots using the window light.

The photographer then laid the newborn on the bed for his portrait, using the dad's T-shirt as a backdrop.

PHOTO NOTES
Making Decisions

Even in the most pressure-packed situations, all sorts of decisions can be made quickly that will increase your chances of success.

✯ Camera Height/Angle

Get up high or down low—don't shoot from the same old position every time.

✯ Lighting

Hunt it down and find it—look for a window and increase your ISO, which will allow you to shoot in lower light.

✯ Depth of Field

If you're up against a distracting background, throw it out of focus with a wide aperture of 2.8, 1.8 or 1.4. (See page 23 for more about depth of field.)

✯ Consecutive Shots

Set your camera to multiple-shot mode. The beauty of digital photography is that you can shoot all you want and not have to pay for the bad prints.

✯ Which Lens?

Experiment with different lenses so that you know which length works best in every situation you find yourself in.

The more you practice, the more second nature this becomes. Before you know it you will become the family photojournalist.

17

Subject

Pushing yourself further as a photographer requires that you learn to look at the world in new and different ways. Consider, then, the difference between the specific and the universal in your images. Challenge yourself to see if there is more than one picture to be had in any given situation. There is almost always a specific image to be taken, but, if you have the eyes to see it, a larger, more universal concept may reveal itself. Once in a while, if you're lucky, you will start out to shoot one subject and through the course of the shoot you will see an entirely different or larger subject emerge. The big picture is always there; it just requires a more developed eye to see it.

Look Beyond the Specific

A specific person at a specific place and time is the stuff of which snapshots are made. There is absolutely nothing wrong with documenting people or scenes in specific ways. Most of the images we will ever take fall into this category. If photos of the specific variety could talk, they would say things like, "Baby Reef, three weeks old" (see photo at right). He's a darling baby and his mom loves this photo, but this isn't an image that would go on a greeting card or on display in a museum.

> "What's interesting is letting people tell you about themselves in the picture."
> — Mary Ellen Mark

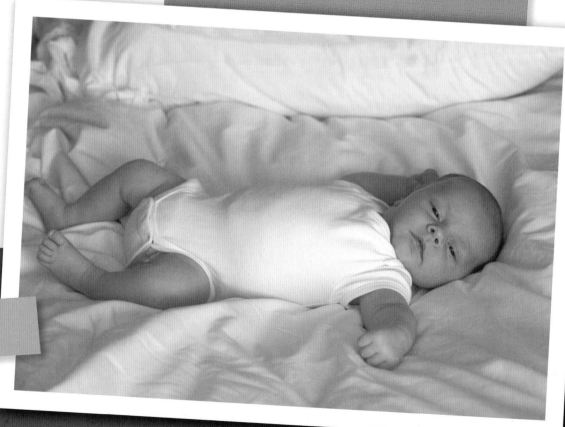

This photo is more specific than universal. It says, "Baby Reef, three weeks old."

Think Universal

Look a little further to see if there is something more to be said, something less concrete that might appeal to anyone looking at the image, regardless of her relationship to the subject. A universally appealing image says something larger and more universal about the subject. If universal images could talk, they would say more abstract and broad things, such as "innocence" or "new."

Instead of "gracie playing dress up," try for an image that says "dream," "imagine" or "wish." You'll know it when you get it.

When you create a universal image, you create art that happens to be your kid. When others view those images, rather than comments about how big your child is getting, you will see an immediate emotional response to the image as it evokes universal emotions that we all have about babies, family and life.

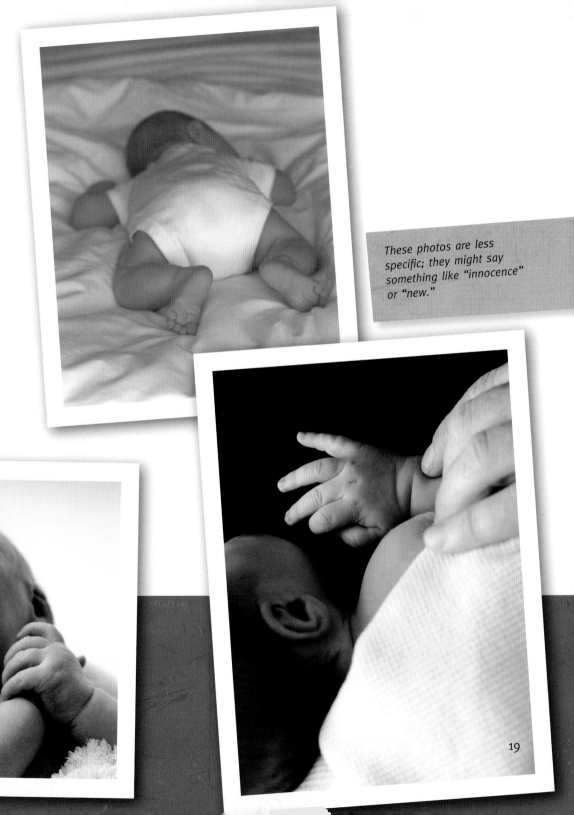

These photos are less specific; they might say something like "innocence" or "new."

19

Janelle Smith

Barb Uil

Kathryn Langford

PHOTO NOTES

Elements for a Universal Photo

There are some common elements that, while not absolute rules, are good starting points for achieving your own more universal images:

1. **A sense of spontaneity in the image** *Catching your subject "in the act." A toddler in mid-stride, mid-swing or mid-pout.*

2. **A glimpse of personality in the subject** *Capturing "that look" he gives you, her turned-up nose, the faint spray of freckles across his cheeks, the mischievous light in her eye—you get the idea.*

3. **A comment or observation about the human condition** *What do you have to say about babies or aging? How can you communicate your feelings visually? What is it you want to say about your subject that will resonate with others who don't know your subject? Using aging as an example, do you want to communicate frailty or weathered strength? What you want to communicate will determine how you take the shot.*

4. **Uncensored emotion** *Will it be the full-out belly laugh, the absolute abandon in a two-year-old's cry or a sneaky tear escaping down dad's cheek as he gives away the bride?*

5. **A slice of intimacy in a relationship** *The interactions between people are of endless fascination. Even if your subjects know they are being photographed, if you are patient and let them relax enough, the relationship will eventually emerge, allowing you to capture it. What will your photo say? Siblings, best friends, competitors?*

6. **Perspective from a "fly on the wall"** *When the subject is unaware of the camera, you can capture moments that would be ruined if you corralled everyone to have their photo taken. Try these: subjects in deep conversation, involved in a project or working, caretaking of another, performing, resting or sleeping.*

7. **A view from behind** *Think about shots where your subject isn't even facing the camera. For example, grandpa and grandson on a walk in the trees from behind, a teenage son with his arm around mom from behind, sisters whispering to each other.*

Emphasize the Subject

When someone looks at your photograph for the first time, there should be no doubt as to the subject of that image. All extraneous "stuff" should be eliminated from the frame so that the only thing left is the subject and what is supporting the subject. There are many ways to draw attention to your subject.

Barb Uil

Barb Uil

Barb Uil

Large in the Frame
By moving in close and making your subject the largest element in the frame, you are leaving no doubt as to what the viewer's focus should be on. This method eliminates distracting backgrounds, simplifying the image.

21

Barb Uil

Frame within a Frame
You can get very literal with this concept, using an actual picture frame or find framing elements in the foreground/background of your environment.

Isolate by Focus
Throwing everything but your subject out of focus makes an interesting statement about what the viewer should be concentrating on.

22

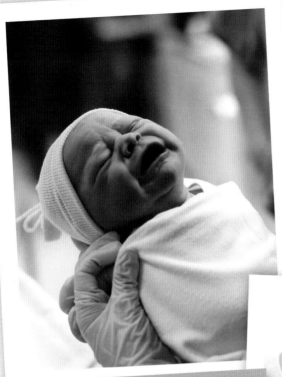

PHOTO NOTES
Blurring the Background

Professional photographers rely on a short depth of field (DOF) to isolate their subjects and throw a distracting background out of focus.

✴ *Long lens (85mm and up)*

✴ *Wide aperture/f-stop (1.4, 1.8, 2.0, 2.8)*

✴ *Get close to subject (physical proximity)*

✴ *Distant background (get them away from the background)*

Color or Lack of Color
Super-saturated color can give more impact to images, or you might have the whole image in black and white and selectively color just one piece. Think of interesting ways to use color to emphasize your subject.

Barb Uil

23

Simplify the Frame

Why is it that some images grab our attention and hang on while others get more lukewarm reactions? More often than not, it is because the attention-getting image has been taken by a photographer who has used one or more compositional rules to simplify the subject.

Create Leading Lines

Studies of human observation have shown that an image that directs the viewer's eye through it will retain the viewer's attention longer. One way to achieve this is by the use of leading lines. A leading line is a line that leads the eye from one place to another within an image.

Amanda Keeys

Actual Lines
Paths, roads, railroad tracks and other leading lines provide a place for our eye to go—denoting the future or a journey ahead.

Imaginary Lines
In this photo of a mother bathing her baby, you could draw a straight line from one to the other by their mutual eye contact. Your eye starts on one and goes back and forth, keeping your attention.

Make Shapes

Learning to look for or create shapes of your subjects can improve your photos dramatically. With groups of people, the best shapes to create are diagonal in nature. Don't stack heads on top of each other, think 'V's and 'W's with heads staggered between one another.

Amanda Keeys

S Curves
Some leading lines are S curves. An S curve leads our eyes to other parts and details of the image and is much more pleasing than a straight-on pose. Women, pregnant and not, and little girls are perfect subjects for exploring the S curve line.

Shapes
To form a harmonious shape in a group of three, the head in the middle should be higher than the two on either side so that the bodies of your subjects form a base for a pleasing triangle shape. The triangle shape allows the eye to move through the image without stopping, which wouldn't be the case if the boys were lined up at the same height.

25

Understand the Rule of Thirds

The "rule of thirds" is based on the concept that the strength of an image improves when the main elements in the photo are placed at key locations away from the center of the frame. Placing the subject away from the center creates visual tension because it is not the way we usually see things. The rule of thirds works in both a horizontal and vertical format. Most of the time if you are shooting a person, the best format will be vertical as we are usually longer than we are wide so a vertical framing follows the obvious vertical line of the body.

We can't honestly say that we shoot thinking, "OK, use the rule of thirds now." But when we've captured something that really zings, it almost invariably has followed the rule of thirds.

Barb Uil

PHOTO NOTES

Work Outside Your Comfort Zone

The easiest way to apply the rule of thirds is to think outside your comfort zone—shoot horizontally when you usually shoot vertically, or vice versa. Or, try some really different cropping. Even if you totally cut off someone's head or completely miss it altogether, it will force you to see in a new way.

Audrey Woulard

Janelle Smith

Kathnyn Langford

Use the rule of thirds when photogaphing more than one subject, uniting them as a unified whole.

Manipulate Scale

Simply stated, scale is the relationship between the size of at least two elements. If you want to draw attention to the size of your subject, small or large, introduce another element or person that will visually illustrate just how big or little they are. This is called providing a sense of scale.

This little girl had a very mature-looking face, and when she was photographed by herself, you couldn't tell how old she was. Standing her in this chair makes it obvious that she's a toddler just by comparing the size of the chair to the child.

To illustrate just how big the dad is in comparison to his little boy, cut him out of the photo altogether, leaving those long legs in to frame the baby.

When shooting outdoors, nature herself provides an environment and brings scale to the image as in this image of two men walking between towering hedges.

Since we all have a general idea of how big a sofa or chair is, furniture is a great element to use when you want to show just how small a baby really is.

PHOTO NOTES
Bits and Pieces

Bits and pieces of babies are so very cute to photograph, but sometimes it can be difficult to appreciate just how precious those tiny tender toes are unless compared to someone or something else we understand the scale of. Using mom or dad as a prop for baby allows us to provide a frame of reference for the size of the baby. Photographing baby feet and hands in comparison to mom or dad's feet and hands gives just the comparison needed to highlight those fragile newborns.

Establish a Viewpoint

The viewpoint we are exploring here is, literally, the view from where you stand. And where you stand is usually not the best viewpoint for the photo you are taking. For example, if you're 5'4" tall and you take every photo from 5'4" your photos will be boring. Crouch down, stand on your tiptoes, hang from a tree, lay on your stomach, do whatever it takes to see things in a different way and to change your viewpoint. You'll love the results.

Barb Uil

Shooting at the subject's eye level gives a feeling of equality.

PHOTO NOTES
Tilting the Camera

For a more commercial, editorial look to your photos, try tilting the camera. Look for the dominant line in the photo (a person standing vertically, a doorway, or the horizon line) and tilt your camera away or toward that line. Note: Watch out for the camera strap dangling in front of your lens!

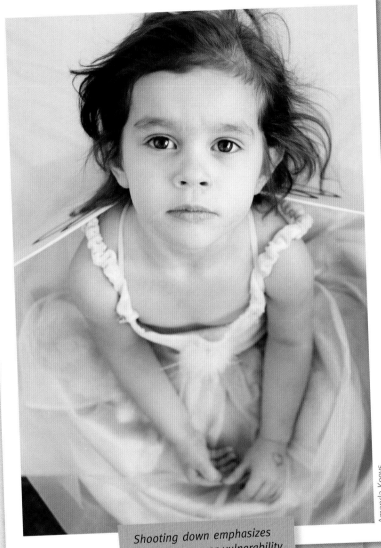

Amanda Keeys

Shooting down emphasizes the innocence or vulnerability of a subject.

Amanda Keeys

Shooting up at subject gives a feeling of power to the subject.

31

Setting

You are surrounded by perfect places to take photos and probably don't even know it. It's tempting to look at photos we admire and think, "Well, sure, I could take pictures like that if I had a great Victorian porch/old barn/fabulous house, etc." Just remember, all you need is a little piece of something interesting as a background and you can take interesting photos anywhere.

Props

Try and select props that are meaningful to the subject rather than something that just looks cute. Does your subject play an instrument or a sport?

Let kids loose in the backyard, and they'll find something cute to do.

Barb Uil

Kim Heffington

Audrey Woulard

32

Outdoors—Natural Settings

Look around your house, neighborhood or town. Keep an eye out for the ratty, old shed in the backyard, a porch step, a tumbling down fence or verandas—any one of these could be a setting for a photo. Don't worry about the laundry in the corner, shoot in close and you'll never see it.

Kathryn Langford

Look for backgrounds that will add interest and texture to the shot.

If you are including it, the setting should tell something about the subject. Choose a place that tells something about their interests or background (beach, mountain, front porch, etc.).

PHOTO NOTES
Location Kit

Keep a small, lightweight backdrop, clamps/bulldog clips and a roll of gaffer tape in your location kit to create last-minute backdrops when the location is unforgiving. Make your own backdrops from dyed sheets, foam core, old rugs or tapestries.

33

Kathryn Langford

Kathryn Langford

Environmental
By adopting the attitude of a photojournalist, you can make images indoors and have them turn out beautifully. The attitude of a photojournalist is to get the shot no matter what it takes; find a way to make the light and the environment work together and get the shot. Crank up the ISO speed on your digital camera or use a really fast speed film (like ISO 1600) and capture the emotion in the shot.

Indoors

When you look through the average person's scrapbook, you don't see a lot of really great photos of kids in their everyday life doing their thing. The reason for this is that, typically, their activities are taking place indoors and photographing indoors can be problematic. Instead, what you see is a lot of over-flashed, poorly composed images that don't convey the feeling of the moment.

Open the doors and the shades and let the light flow in through the window; you now have an indoor studio.

PHOTO NOTES
Forget the Flash!

Indoors, a flash is sometimes the only way to get the shot, but don't treat it as the first choice. Try some of the tips listed here before you turn on the flash. And when it comes to indoor events, such as recitals or sporting events, forget the flash altogether. All the flash will get you is a perfectly exposed photo of the back of someone's head while the stage or the court is a patch of black.

Events

Some of the more challenging photographic situations are indoor events, from basketball games to school plays. When you're far away and forbidden to use flash, how can you get a decent shot of your kid as the star? The best bet is to use a fast lens (maximum aperture of 2.8 or higher) and high ISO (both of these images were shot at a very high ISO of 1000 or higher).

35

Share the Story

Some photographers have a style that is rich in beauty, while others are born storytellers. Telling a story in an image is a challenge as any photojournalist will tell you. For photojournalists, the story comes first and everything else takes a backseat. They aren't particularly concerned about grainy images or the perfect pose. Catching the story as it unfolds is their only concern.

Exceptional story-telling photos tap into our universal understanding of the human condition. Even if we don't know the particular story of that image, an emotionally evocative image will cause us to construct our own story about it.

Symbols

The things we love tell a story about who we are. Using symbols in your work can be as literal as photographing grandpa's pocket watch in the hands of the grandson or as abstract as using certain symbols that are significant to you or your subject in the images you capture. Some photographers enjoy photographing similar types of symbols throughout their career, symbols such as hands or feet, eyes or other parts and pieces. What are the symbols in your life?

Ruth Giauque

Emotion

Look through any collection of Pulitzer Prize-winning photographs and you will see, in almost every case, raw emotion. While not every photo we take will evoke an emotional response from others, our best work will.

Janelle Smith

It is often in the parts and pieces of images that we find or imagine the story. The photographer shoots an image that leaves us wanting more. We are left to imagine the details of where, who and why. There are stories in everyday images, life that is shot in the moment, captured because our hearts and our vision act as one.

Barb Uil

Taking advantage of great windows and plain white bedding, the photographer backs away, just outside the door to capture an intimate and emotional portrait of a brand-new family.

37

Daily Life

Most times we are so close to our daily life that we don't see the beauty in or the fleeting nature of it. Photos of the tasks and activities of the everyday may well end up being the photos that are most precious to us years from now.

It won't be long before those toddlers at the table become teenagers grabbing a snack as they run out the door. Capture dinnertime in all its glory.

Barb Uil

38

PHOTO NOTES
The Photo Essay

So much information can be gathered from a photo, but it is a rare event that can be completely explained in just one image. Weddings, births, birthdays, graduations, holidays—all of these occasions and more are perfect opportunities for creating a photo essay. When planning to create a photo essay, keep the following points in mind:

⭐ **Pick a theme** Just like any story, a photo essay should revolve around a central theme that will tie all of the images together.

⭐ **Show a story arc** Be sure you capture the beginning, middle and ending of the event. This will also help portray the passage of time. Definitely be ready to capture the climax and the defining moments.

⭐ **Determine point-of-view** As the photographer, are you on the outside looking in? Or, are you telling the story through another's eyes (such as a mom-to-be, who is about to give birth)? You can also shift the point-of-view throughout your photo documentation by photographing events from the level of another, such as the knee-high view of a small child or pet or from above to show the watchful eye of a father.

⭐ **Develop the characters** Every story has characters. Spend time documenting each character in your story. Don't interrupt them—you want to capture the reality. Ask them to pose when there is a lull in activity.

⭐ **Convey mood** Be ready to capture expressions, gestures, body language and exchanges between your characters.

⭐ **Define the details** Look for the symbols in your story. If you are photographing a family holiday, be sure to photograph special ornaments or holiday serving platters that have been passed down through time.

39

The Four 'M's of Lighting

"...through this photographic eye you will be able to look out on a new light-world, a world for the most part uncharted and unexplored, a world that lies waiting to be discovered and revealed." — Edward Weston

Light is the medium in which a photographer works. Painters apply paint, and sculptors chip away at stone while the photographer manipulates light. However, not all light is created equal. Some light is harsh and unflattering, while other light seems to caress the subject, making the viewer feel as if she can reach out and touch the texture in the image. For a new photographer, it is difficult to see how light and shadow translate into the final image. In fact, one of the single biggest factors separating more experienced photographers from beginning photographers is the way that they consider the light falling on their subjects.

The beginning photographer shoots away, with flash or without, in full sun or in shade, more concerned about the quantity rather than the quality of the light. The more experienced photographer takes a moment before picking up her camera to consider the following about the light in any given setting:

MAIN LIGHT ❯ *The first thing a skilled photographer will do is determine the light source he will use to light the photograph. It might be the sun shining through a doorway or window or the more controlled studio strobe light.*

METER THE SCENE ❯ *Using a light meter, the photographer will then determine if there is enough light to record the image.*

MOOD ❯ *Once she has determined that the quantity of light is sufficient, the photographer then considers whether or not the quality of light will achieve the mood or feeling she is seeking to convey in the image.*

MODIFY THE SITUATION ❯ *The photographer will then determine how to position the subject to best take advantage of the lighting situation. If, after all this decision-making, the light still is not right, it might be necessary for the photographer to fine tune by modifying the light in some way.*

Only after these decisions have been made is it time to shoot. Follow along as we explore, in detail, the decision-making process that every photographer must navigate in order to exploit the medium of light.

41

Main Light

It might seem obvious, but the first step in the making of any photograph is finding a light source, known in the photo world as the main light or sometimes the key light. When shooting outdoors, the main light will most likely be sunlight. The sun is the ultimate light source and, used properly, could be the only light you'll ever need or use. Yet, while the sun can provide a great quantity of light, the quality might not always be what you're looking for. This is why you need to learn how to hunt for good light.

Indirect Light vs. Direct Light

When starting out, it's a good idea to avoid DIRECT sunlight. Direct sunlight (defined as the rays of the sun directly touching your subject) can be very intense, casting harsh shadows and causing your subject to squint. Instead, look for INDIRECT light; light that is bounced off, diffused through or partially blocked by something else.

42

A perfect example of the soft, even light provided by a porch overhang, this photo of two siblings could easily expand to include the entire family, all perfectly lit by indirect light.

Audrey Woulard

INDIRECT LIGHT

Photographers love working with indirect light because its diffused quality results in soft and even lighting. It naturally complements skin tones by eliminating harsh shadows and reducing the appearance of blemishes. Indirect light can be found most anywhere if you know what to look for.

Open Shade and Overcast Days Open shade is an open patch of sky that provides soft, even illumination without the harsh shadows of direct light. It is called open shade because there is nothing blocking the light from above, which is what differentiates it from the shade provided by a garage or porch overhang. The most common type of open shade would be an overcast day. The clouds in an overcast sky act as a huge diffuser for the light of the sun, evening out shadows and giving you a giant "studio" to work in. On sunny days, the shady sides of buildings and the shadows produced by trees are excellent sources of open shade.

Porches/Garages Overhangs like porches and garages are ideal for lighting one or many people. Many times the walkway up to a house acts as a reflector throwing light into the subjects' faces.

Kathryn Langford

In this unusual photo of a little girl on the beach, you can see that she is in open shade with light coming from overhead. The light is diffused, preventing harsh shadows from appearing on the little girl.

Amanda Keevs

In this photo of a boy in the park, you can see that the surrounding trees form a pocket of gorgeous light.

Audrey Woulard

You can see in the left portion of this photo that this is a very bright day. Positioning the girl against the shady side of the building in open shade softly and evenly illuminates her without exposing her to the glaring midday light.

43

PHOTO NOTES

Sunrise, Sunset: The Golden Hour

The golden hour is one hour before sunset. The late afternoon sun shines through the dust in the air turning the light golden. The golden light of late afternoon sun is highly sought after by natural light photographers. The benefit of shooting at the beginning or end of day is that the light is not straight overhead (which causes raccoon eyes) but coming at an angle, which is more flattering.

The Old Farmer's Almanac Web site, www.almanac. com/rise/locations/index.php, has sunrise and sunset times for your area.

DIRECT LIGHT

Direct light isn't necessarily bad, but it does require a little practice to get it right. If your only option is to shoot in direct sunlight, make an effort to keep your subject's face out of the light. (Carefully read the section on metering, pages 50–53, to get your exposure right and keep the sun to the side or back of your subject.)

Janelle Smith

This photo was taken in direct sunlight. The photographer exposed for the face of her subject allowing the highlights in her hair to "blow," which means to go bright and lose detail. The effect is a rim of light around the subject that avoids harsh shadows on her face.

44

PHOTO NOTES

When you're shooting outside, watch out for lens flare—those funky little blobs of light in your images that come from the sun skimming off the surface of your lens. Sometimes there are no blobs, but everything in your image shows up as too light and slightly hazy. Notice in the bottom image the light blobs in the upper right corner and on the parents. The flare has also caused a haze over the entire image, resulting in low contrast. A lens shade will prevent lens flare (if your lens didn't come with one, you can purchase them at your local camera store). Sometimes even a lens shade won't work. In that case, ask someone to block the light from hitting your lens, or use your free hand to block the light.

If you like the look of lens flare and want to use it in a creative way, experiment until you achieve pleasing results. Take off your lens shade, allow the sun to hit the side of your lens and watch for the flare in your viewfinder. The photographer of the photo shown at right incorporated a bit of lens flare in the upper right corner to enhance the mood of golden sunshine.

Warning: Never look at the sun through any lens—it could cause eye damage.

The image at right illustrates good, creative use of lens flare. The image below illustrates poor lens flare.

45

Janelle Smith

Hunting for Light

Fabulous natural light is easy to find, once you know where to look. For starters, walk around your home to see if there aren't at least one or two places to try. While you're doing the dishes, watch how the light falls on your soap dispenser. Notice how the light changes in your home throughout the day. Do you have really big windows, fabulous doorways or porch overhangs that give you gorgeous light every time? Start taking mental notes of places and let us introduce you to the soon-to-be-famous Front Door Studio.

THE FRONT DOOR STUDIO

The Front Door Studio was born out of sheer laziness. We needed to take bridal photos of a friend's daughter and just couldn't get in the mood to set up all those studio lights. As Allison sent her kids off to school that morning, she noticed that the light coming through her front door looked really nice and an idea was born. "Why not take the bridal portrait in the entryway?" And so we did.

We started by looking at the light both inside and out. The door faces east and it was morning, so the light outside of the door was very direct and harsh. But just inside the door and in the entryway, it was divine.

46

We positioned our bride-to-be in the doorway; you can see here how close she is to the light. Direct light is just outside the door so we had to be careful to keep her just inside, allowing maximum light, but keeping it indirect.

Setting our ISO a little higher, we ventured into the entryway to allow the bride to sit down for some headshots.

47

THE WINDOW LIGHT STUDIO

Window light is one of the most beautiful forms of lighting there is. A window provides a box of light and, depending on how you position your subject, you can capture some of the most beautiful images you ever imagined. Depending on the direction the window is facing, you can get a very light, airy effect, or a more subdued moody feel.

Window Light Setup
This is just one of many ways to set up a window-light portrait. In regard to the proximity of the window, notice where the camera and the subject's chair are located. The window is facing north, so it has even light throughout the day. With east-facing windows, you may want to shoot in the afternoon to avoid direct sunlight. With west-facing windows, morning is best.

This image of a young boy was taken with the drapes on the window pulled closed to allow just a shaft of light to illuminate the boy.

Audrey Woulard

The simplicity of the background and the soft, gorgeous light allows the photographer to spend her time focusing on getting the perfect expression from her subject rather than worrying about her camera settings.

THE TUB LIGHT STUDIO

It's a not-very-well-kept secret among location photographers that bathrooms are sometimes the best places for gorgeous light. Many bathrooms have fabulous glass block windows that refract light all over the place, and if the bathroom is painted white, the light bounces and fills the room with gorgeous, indirect light. Check out the light in your bathroom.

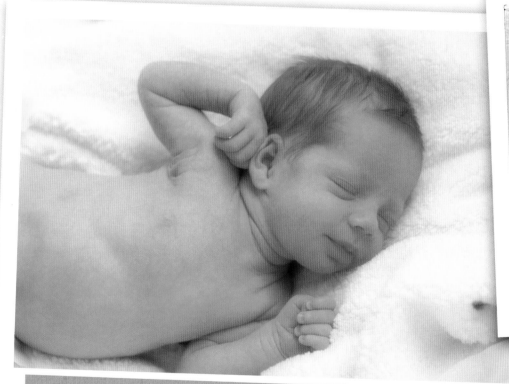

Audrey Woulard

You'd never think that this fashion-conscious boy was sitting on the edge of his mom's bathtub would you? Careful metering for the boy's face (see pages 50–53) allowed the background light to "blow," and the white walls in front of the boy reflected soft, even light back onto his face.

The photographer placed fluffy blankets in the bottom of the master bathtub. The tub sits below a south-facing glass block window. Add a baby, and you're ready to shoot away with all the gorgeous light any photographer could want.

Meter

With the advent of digital photography, it is tempting to just shoot and see if you "got it" on the camera monitor. And if you really didn't "get it," you might be able to fix it up in Photoshop. But your goal should always be to get the best images possible straight out of the camera. So whether you're shooting film or digital, it is critical to understand how to expose an image properly. To do that, you must understand how to use a light meter. Knowing how to use a light meter correctly will forever change your photos and, dare we say, your life.

Exposure

The books that have been written on exposure could fill a library, but it all comes down to a simple little concept that Goldilocks figured out a long time ago: Exposure is capturing an image that is not too light and not too dark, but just right. How we get that image is by using a light meter.

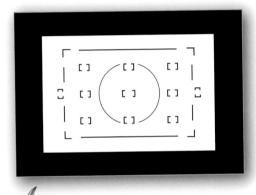

Reflected Light Meters
(a.k.a. the Meter in Your Camera)

The meter in your camera is a reflected light meter. Reflected light meters measure the light that is reflected off of your subject. For average scenes (not too light and not too dark), the Auto exposure programs on your camera will do just fine, but what really separates the girls from the women in the photo world is the ability to precisely meter any scene for accurate exposure.

Your Camera's Viewfinder
(a.k.a. Mission Control)

When you look through the viewfinder of any camera, you will notice that there are several brackets, lights going on and off and numbers here and there. Guess what? In order to take correctly exposed, in-focus photos, you need to know what those brackets, lights and numbers are and what they can do for you. So, get out your manual and determine which of those brackets is your exposure meter. The reflected light exposure meter is typically in the center of the frame. It might look like little brackets or, possibly, a circle with crosshairs. When you look through the viewfinder and center this bracket on something, you are telling the camera that you want that portion of the scene correctly exposed.

This photo is a great example of a scene that needs a meter reading. Taken on Auto the background would have been much lighter and the girl's face in shadow. By taking a meter reading and setting her camera manually, the photographer got the exposure dead on.

Barb Uil

→ REFLECTED LIGHT METER TECHNIQUE

1. Assuming an ISO of 400, set your camera to "auto" mode. Fill your frame with the most important part of the scene you are photographing. (The reason you fill the frame with the face of your subject is so that nothing else in the scene will affect the exposure of the face.) If it is a portrait of a person, the most important part is usually the face. Looking through your viewfinder, place the exposure bracket on the face of the person (or the most important part of the subject) you are photographing and press the shutter release halfway down—this will result in a meter reading that will show up in your viewfinder to give you a recommended f-stop and shutter speed for correct exposure. Remember these numbers—let's say it's f8 at 125 of a second.

2. Set your camera to Manual and your aperture to f8 and shutter to 125.

Don't forget to change your settings if your scene or the lighting changes.

3. You are ready to shoot and, unless you move your subject or the lighting changes (due to weather, cloud cover, etc.) you won't need to change your settings.

51

Using an off-camera, incident light meter is the most accurate way to determine the correct exposure. Because incident light meters measure the light falling on the subject (also called the ambient, or available light), these meters aren't fooled by extremes in light or dark skin or clothing. If you are a serious photo enthusiast or considering photography as a business, an incident light meter is an essential tool. Remember when we talked earlier about "hunting for light"? Well, when you go hunting for light, you should hunt with an incident light meter.

→ BASIC INCIDENT LIGHT METER TECHNIQUE

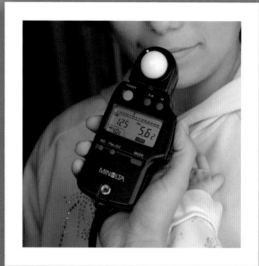

This technique involves metering for the subject. By holding the meter in the subject's position, facing the camera, and dialing in those numbers to your camera, you are, in effect, saying, "This is the most important area in the photograph. This is the part that I want exposed perfectly."

1. Dial the ISO you would like to use into the meter, in this case 400 ISO.

2. Place your meter where your subject will be, with the dome facing the camera position, and take a reading. Let's say you have a reading of f-5.6 at 125/sec.

3. Set your camera to manual and your aperture to the same settings as your reading.

4. You are ready to shoot and, unless you move your subject or the lighting changes (due to weather, cloud cover, etc.) you won't need to change your settings.

PHOTO NOTES

The Trifecta of Good Exposure

What if you just can't get enough light? It is important to remember that when things are getting dark and blurry, you have three options to allow more light into your camera and save the exposure.

Wider aperture The wider you open your lens, the more light can enter. This is where the "faster lenses" with maximum apertures of 2.8, 1.8 or even 1.4 can really shine. Just remember when you're working with a wide aperture, your depth of field will be very shallow, so focusing properly is critical.

Higher ISO On a digital camera, increasing your ISO is as easy as the push of a button. Just remember that the higher the speed, the more digital "noise" you may experience. Digital noise is similar to grain in film.

Slower shutter speed This tip is last because it's the one that can get you into the most trouble. Slowing down your shutter speed will allow more light into your camera but, if you set it too slow, you're going to get blur from camera movement or the movement of your subject or both! A good rule of thumb if you are hand holding your camera (which means NOT on a tripod) is to set your shutter speed NO SLOWER than the focal length of your lens. For example: If you are shooting with a 28-80 zoom lens, to be on the safe side, your shutter speed shouldn't be set any slower than 1/80 of a second. If your camera is set on a tripod, you only have to worry about the movement of your subject.

When working in extremely backlit conditions, it is essential to have an incident meter to determine the correct exposure.

53

Mood

Unlike any other variable, light has the ability to infuse a photograph with emotion. Aptly manipulated, it will empower an image to cause an onlooker to linger. It will add texture and dimension. To use light to its maximum benefit, you must be able to identify with your subject. Who is this person, and how should she be conveyed? Pre-visualize the shots to help harness the desired result. For example, photographing a sweet newborn baby will require a very different approach to lighting than, say, capturing the essence of a fashion-conscious teenager. Once you begin to develop your interpretive sense of lighting, you'll see your creativity soar.

"A passionate photographer is also an artist. She can photograph what she sees and put feeling and mood into it. She has done it so well that each person that views it will feel their own emotion from it, not just what she saw and felt. No one should walk away feeling nothing."
— Marsha Cairo

The Key of Light

One way of conveying mood is to shoot photos in a particular "key" of light. Similar to a score of music being composed in a particular key, the key in which you light a photograph can have a dramatic effect on the mood of your final image.

HIGH KEY

A high-key image is made up of predominantly light tones. The light is generally very diffused with little or no shadows, and the background and surroundings (and sometimes even the clothing) are all very light in a high-key photo. The darkest part of a high-key photo is the skin tones so the emphasis is on the face, or the shape of the subject. High-key photography is used extensively in advertising with all white backgrounds to avoid any distraction from the product being sold.

Audrey Woulard

This informal family portrait makes use of a bedroom with lots of light and white walls. The look is fresh and natural.

Shooting parts of a subject in high key can give a magazine-quality feel to an image like this one of a little girl's cowboy boots.

High-key lighting can project a contemporary fashion-forward feel like this portrait of a young girl. With floor-to-ceiling patio doors behind the subject, the photographer metered for the girl's face and let the background blow out.

LOW KEY

An image set in low-key lighting is comprised of primarily dark tones. Much like the paintings of Rembrandt, who portrayed many of his subjects in dark rooms lit by a single window or door opening, a low-key image typically has lighting that is very directional with strong highlights and shadows. Low-key images tend to have an "artsy" feel to them.

Just as a highly backlit space can serve well for high-key images, a space with restricted light coming in by either a window or door can serve well for a low-key image. Since the surrounding environment and sometimes even the clothing is dark, the skin and the face become the focus of the image.

For a different take on the dreamy and romantic mood, this photographer posed her daughter in a dark dress against a field of dark foliage. Allowing the light to outline her against the dark background provided a romantic, otherworldly feel.

Amanda Keeys

Low-key lighting is a nice change of pace for child portrait with an artsy feel. By the way, do you recognize those boots? They were shown on the previous spread. It's the same little girl, just in a different light.

Low-key lighting also works well for this tightly cropped family portrait of a couple with its new baby. This photo was achieved by placing a black backdrop on the wall of a balcony outside a hotel room and positioning the new family in front of it for some low-key shots.

Modify

Taking the best photos demands that a photographer be flexible in the face of less-than-ideal circumstances and be willing to take wild chances in the hope of getting something great. The reason that more experienced photographers get better images is because they've done the trial and error (with heavy emphasis on the errors) and figured out what works, what doesn't and what to do when something isn't working.

This section will cover refinements on the concepts you've learned so far. It will also explain how to fix things when the lighting is wrong. The modifications are most often small and subtle, but they make all the difference in the final image.

Direction of Light on Location

Remember when we said that the difference between good and bad light depends on where you stand? This is especially true when working with light on location. The images shown here illustrate how important this point is.

This image was taken outside under a porch overhang. The girl was placed with the light direction coming from the left side (the photographer's left). This wrap-around effect of light and shadow gives a 3-D effect to her face.

In this image the photographer pointed the girl's face into the light, opening up the shadows, flattening out the light and giving a more fashion or glamour look to the shot. Neither treatment is right or wrong; they're just different. If you were photographing an older woman, the more flattering shot would be the flat lighting.

FLAT

A flat-lit photo is one of the easier lighting techniques. Find a doorway, garage or other overhang and place your subject face-on into the light while you stand in front of her in the light. Flat lighting is flattering to everyone and a good choice for group shots or an older person who doesn't want his wrinkles to show.

3-D REMBRANDT

To achieve a more three-dimensional feel, just reposition your subject. Place your subject at a 45- to 90-degree angle to the same light source that you used for flat lighting and, voila! You have Rembrandt lighting.

This image takes advantage of the flat light provided by placing the subject under a porch overhang and facing her into the light.

The 3-dimensional, Rembrandt effect is achieved by placing this young man on a porch and turning his face at an angle to the light.

This flat-lit shot was taken by facing the subject into the indirect light.

Audrey Woulard

Audrey Woulard

Audrey Woulard

59

Direction of Light in the Studio

Experimenting with direction and angle of light is most easily demonstrated in a studio. The beauty of using studio light is you have complete control. You can place your subject and then move the light wherever you want. There are many excellent books that exhaustively cover the subject of studio lighting. For this section, we want to give you just a little taste of what is possible with a single light, if you are so inclined.

Studio Lights

Whether you are working with studio strobe or hot lights, the best way to start is with one or, at the most, two lights. If you have been outdoors looking for and working with natural light, you'll be a step ahead when you head into the studio because you will already know what lighting angles work the best. The angles are no different in the studio; the difference is that you can control the direction by actually moving the light around.

HOT LIGHTS

Hot lights are known as a "continuous light source," which is to say, big light bulbs with more power than the ones you use in your house lamps. One advantage to hot lights is that they don't flash, which is nice when you don't want to startle your subjects (as when working with newborns). They are less expensive than studio strobes, and the light source is continuous so it is easier to see the light you are getting than it is with studio strobe lights.

The downside of hot lights is that they are, well, hot. Care must be taken with any reflectors or diffusers so as not to burn down your house. Hot lights also tend to have a very warm colorcast to them, which can be easily compensated for by changing your white balance to a tungsten setting. (Check your camera's manual for the white balance settings for each lighting situation you find yourself in.) The hot lights' warm temperature of light can be a plus if you are looking for a warm yellow or orange glow.

→ # HOT LIGHT SETUP

The hot light setup is probably the easiest place to start when experimenting with studio lighting. The lights you see in this setup are inexpensive photographic hot lights. A makeshift background stand can be made from a broom handle and two chairs or, if you're handy, PVC pipe.

Warning! Hot lights are very hot and can cause fire. Use caution when working with them, especially around children.

1. If using two lights, place both lights together (to act as one, big light source) behind a white bed sheet (which doesn't have to be ironed!) clamped to a background stand.

2. Meter the light using either the reflected meter (in camera) or incident meter (off camera) technique (see pages 50–53).

3. You can see that the big light source we are trying to create makes a wall of light to the left of where we are going to have our subject sitting.

4. Place a bit of black cloth behind where the subject's head will be to give the portrait a low-key feel to it. Note that you don't need a whole, huge black backdrop if you are just doing a head shot as we are here.

5. And here are the results. You can see that the hot lights did provide quite a warm color cast to the image, but converting it to black and white in Photoshop eliminated the need to worry about color issues.

STUDIO STROBE

Studio strobes are essentially really big off-camera flashes. The speed at which a strobe flashes allows it to freeze the action of your subject, which is great when shooting fast-moving subjects, like kids. The quality of light from a studio strobe tends to be a bit more "sparkly" and crisp than natural light. The downside to studio strobe lights is the expense (a bit pricey). You'll also need an incident flash meter to use them properly because, unlike with hot lights or natural light, what you see is not what you are going to get. Since the flash of the strobe happens so quickly, you won't know whether you are getting a correct exposure unless you use an incident meter.

STUDIO STROBE SETUP

A studio strobe setup requires a few more steps and more equipment, but we'll give you a sense of how it's done here. You can see the progression of the setup during this shoot of a newborn baby.

1. First, meter the strobe to get an exposure setting for the camera, then set your camera to manual and dial in the settings from the meter.

2. You can see here how small an area is needed to get the shot.

3. With the strobe light on the right side and foam core reflectors all around, plus the white baby blanket, this is set up to be a high-key portrait of a newborn baby.

4. Position the baby at an angle to the light and shoot away.

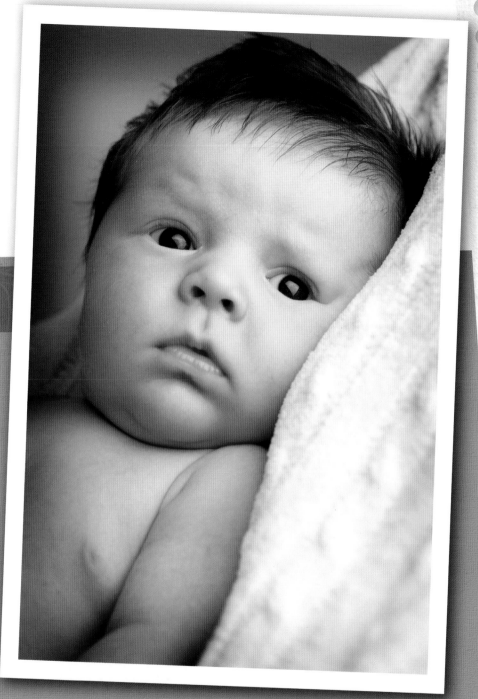

5. And here are the results.

PHOTO NOTES
Check the Eyes for Clues

If you find an image you like in a book or magazine, it's not too hard to tell how it was taken and what kind of lighting setup was used. It's all in the eyes.

If you look closely in this little boy's eye, you can see the photographer and the position of the light being used. Look back through your inspiration file of images and see if you can make out how each photograph was lit by checking the reflections in the eyes of the subjects. You might even see the photographer herself!

Proximity

One concept that just blew us away when we were first leaning the ins and outs of lighting was the proximity of the light sources to the subjects. The photographers we observed had their subjects right up against their light sources. It was then that we learned a vital lighting fact: The closer the light source is to the subject, the more diffused it becomes. This seems counterintuitive: Wouldn't the light being closer make it harsher? It seems so, but it's not.

As you look through the photos in this book you will notice that, in almost every case, the subject is right "on the edge" of direct light and just inside a pocket of nice, indirect lighting. The same holds true for light in-studio. The studio light is *very* close to the subject, keeping the shadows from getting too harsh and wrapping gorgeous light all around them such as this window-lit portrait of a little girl on her mother's lap. She is positioned right on the window to maximize the light.

Remember: Get your subject as close to the light as you possibly can without having the rays of direct light touching her.

CATCHLIGHTS

The eyes are not only the windows to the soul, they are great indicators of whether or not the light is working for your subject. Those beautiful reflections that add sparkle and life to the eyes are called catchlights. They're not absolutely essential; if it comes to a choice between an image with great emotion vs. the perfectly lit eyes, go for the emotion every time. That being said, it is still useful to know how to get catchlights in your subject's eyes.

Audrey Woulard

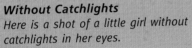

Without Catchlights
Here is a shot of a little girl without catchlights in her eyes.

Uneven Catchlights
With light in one eye but not the other, the other can look dead and flat.

With Catchlights
Lighting both eyes properly adds a sparkle to the portrait. Orienting your subject toward the main light, either in studio or on location, provides beautiful catchlights.

Light Modifiers

Sometimes you will find that you are required to shoot in less-than-perfect conditions: the beach at noon, an east-facing window in the morning, you get the idea. It is at these times that knowing how to modify the light you do have can make all the difference.

There are all kinds of pricey gadgets on the market for modifying light but we've found that learning to search for light modifiers within the environment allows you to be more creative and less a slave to equipment.

Recognizing that light modifiers are designed to perform three basic tasks will give you a head start on taking advantage of light modifiers in any environment.

DIFFUSION

A diffuser is placed between direct light and your subject, softening harsh shadows and producing a more even, flattering light. If the only window you have has harsh, direct light streaming through it, pull sheer drapes, tack up a white sheet or pop a diffuser in the window to diffuse the light on your subject.

A diffuser can be a sheer drapery like the one used in the portrait at right of an expectant couple. Other diffusers we have used include white sheets (using white will avoid inadvertently casting a color on your image), white cheesecloth and scrim material available at fabric stores. You can also purchase a commercial diffuser from a camera store and use it on location when the sun is too direct, as in the photo of the boy shown here.

Kathryn Langford

REFLECTION

A reflector reflects the main light back into the shadowy areas of an image, opening them up and keeping them from becoming too harsh. White foamcore is a tried and true reflector for many photographers.

Kim Heffington

Even simpler than foamcore is someone in a white T-shirt standing close to your subject. In this senior portrait, the photographer took advantage of the white wall the girl was leaning against to reflect some light back into her face.

Kathryn Langford

This soon-to-be-mother has beautiful light reflected into her face by her white pajamas and the white sofa she is sitting on.

Audrey Woulard

BLOCKING

Sometimes you just need to block the light from your subject or part of the scene you are photographing. The most common reasons for blocking light are to block light from hitting a background, to block light from reaching one side of your subject or to block light from reflecting off a surface. Black foamcore is a great light blocker, but a shady side of a building or a darkly painted wall can serve to block light too. In the photo of a young boy, you can see how the two walls on both sides of him sort of "swallow up" the light leaving him lit from in front.

If you are shooting at midday on a cloudy day, even though the clouds are diffusing the light, it is still directional from above and can cause "raccoon eyes." In this case, the brim of the little girl's hat blocks the overhead light keeping the lighting on her face soft and even. Other blocking devices can be porch overhangs or doorways. (Remember all those places that we searched for light?)

Audrey Woulard

PHOTO NOTES
Do-or-Die Lighting

Sometimes you are in a do-or-die situation—the beach at noon with nary a diffuser in sight, or a birthday party in a dim, dark kitchen. Not every shot is going to be a set-up photo shoot; we all have lives and want to document them with a minimum of fuss. Still you want to get a nice shot and avoid over-flashed or underexposed images, so what can you do?

For too-dark situations:

Turn it on Try to raise the ambient light level, which is just photo-speak for turning on as many lights in the room as you can.

Crank it up On a digital camera crank your ISO up as high as you can or use a really fast film (i.e. ISO 800 or higher) to avoid using on-camera flash straight on to your subject.

Bounce the light If you must flash, and your flash head can be turned, try to bounce the flash off the ceiling or a nearby wall. If not, try taping a piece of white vellum tracing paper or tissue to the front of your flash to diffuse it just a bit.

Fill it up When all else fails, try using the fill flash setting on your camera rather than the auto flash setting to give you a less intense burst of flash and allow the light in the setting to show through like this twilight photo of a couple at the Eiffel Tower. Note: Not all cameras have a fill flash setting.

For too bright situations:

Fill flash Fill flash is especially helpful when there are harsh shadows present or when all the light is coming from behind your subject. Consult your manual and find the fill flash setting for your camera. Though this seems counterintuitive, "Why do I want to add more light to an already bright scene?" using the fill flash as a reflector or fill light keeps the shadows from becoming too harsh, and fills in the raccoon shadows in the eyes caused by overhead lighting. Fill flash saved this travel portrait from becoming a silhouette against the skyscrapers.

Austin Smylie

Austin Smylie

69

Image Gallery

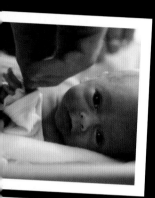

Amanda Keeys

Kathryn Langford

The following pages are a gift of pure inspiration. The image gallery begins by highlighting the stages of human life—featuring subjects ranging from expectant parents to children, young adults and entire families. The gallery is designed to provide a visual feast of images, which in turn should spark ideas for photo shoots of your own.

As you discover your creative process, begin from a place of emotion. Instead of stressing about f-stops and shutter speeds, breathe deeply and think about the feelings or ideas you want your images to convey. The Show the Emotion heading in each spread signals a list of descriptive words to inspire meaningful images as well as a list of shots both obvious and unusual that you will want to try.

You'll also find Creative Challenges that dare you to implement the techniques you learned in the earlier sections of this book with specific methods and approaches tailored to your particular subject. And the gallery's four Photo Art sections explore cool and interesting ideas for using the photos you have taken as display pieces in your home.

Janelle Smith

Maternity

Carrying a child is a life-altering experience for every woman. The changing shape of that gorgeous belly is an event to be celebrated and photographed. Ever since Demi Moore posed pregnant on the cover of *Vanity Fair* magazine, a maternity portrait has become de rigeur for most expectant moms. Whether it's your first child or your last, the pending arrival of a new baby is an exciting time for all concerned. The growing belly garners attention wherever mom goes. Capture the joy of this time and the anticipation of everyone in the family.

Creative Challenge

Include the dad-to-be Introducing the dad-to-be into the photo can give the feel of protection and strength. He can be a prominent element or act as a frame to the pregnant mother. The contrast between the dad's masculine, hairy arms and the soft, smooth skin of the mom's rounded belly are a beautiful contrast.

Photograph from a new angle By photographing the mother and child facing away from the camera, the feel of the image becomes more universal.

Relax self-conscious moms If you are dealing with a mom who's a bit self-conscious about being photographed, try shooting her dressed in black against a black background with just her tummy poking out. Add in the father to enfold her in his arms and you have a flattering portrait that any new mom will love.

Keep a record Establish a spot in your home and take a photo of the mother-to-be in the same place and in the same pose every month to document the growth of the new baby.

Capture the curves You don't have to get the "whole mom" in every photo. Use just the belly or parts of it for a more abstract, interpretive shot. Remember: If you are going to be photographing the belly bare, have the mom wear loose clothing so the elastic marks from her clothing don't show in the photograph.

Janelle Smith

SHOW THE
Emotion

Think of meaningful feelings or concepts you'd like to illustrate with your photo: ripeness, abundance, expectation, anticipation, miracle, love, joy, protection.

SHOTS TO TRY:

Dad's hands on mom's belly ✴ *Older sibling listening to or kissing mom's tummy* ✴ *Parts and pieces of the mom's curvaceous body* ✴ *Mom looking at the camera, away from camera* ✴ *Window-lit shot with natural light to give texture* ✴ *Shots outdoors in nature or on the beach* ✴ *Mom reclining on her side in a cushy chair* ✴ *Profile of the tummy to emphasize the curve* ✴ *Tummy naked* ✴ *Tummy covered with form-fitting tank top* ✴ *Mom naked with side view* ✴ *More than one prego: pregnant sisters or friends* ✴ *In the hospital before delivery*

73

Newborns

"Miraculous" doesn't begin to describe the feeling of holding a newborn baby. This little breath of humanity has been worried over, dreamed about and anticipated for much longer than just nine months. It is one of the most amazing facets of human nature, and by the time a new baby makes an appearance, everyone is instantly, irrevocably and unconditionally in love with him. The world is new again and all possibilities lie ahead for this new little one. A newborn is, technically, only considered a newborn for the first three weeks of life. This period, called the neonatal period, lasts from birth to three weeks. This is the time when they "look" like newborns, fuzzy ears, wrinkly skin and all. Babies at this stage change almost hourly, so it is important to capture this phase.

Creative Challenge

Take hospital shots If you can, snap a few shots in the hospital to document the baby's entry into the world.

Use parents as props Make it a priority to portray the emotion between parent and child by using the parent as a prop for the baby. Lay the baby over the mom's shoulder or in the dad's arms and focus on the baby framed by the parent. Or show off the small scale of baby parts by putting their feet or a hand into dad's hands.

Forget the outfits For a newborn shoot, try to discourage the "outfit" mentality. Newborns don't look good in blue jeans, suits or any other "big people" clothing. Capture what makes them unique at this time by focusing in on their tiny fingers and toes or the reflexes that will fade with time. For best results, save the outfits and the huge headbands for when the baby is a bit older.

Let them sleep Take advantage of the fact that most newborns sleep a lot. Don't try to wake them up. At this stage, their eyes don't focus and you can get a kind of weird staring look. A sleeping baby is universally appealing.

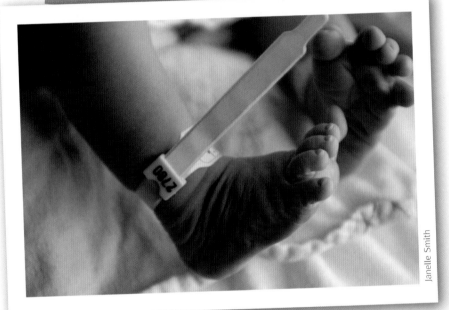

Janelle Smith

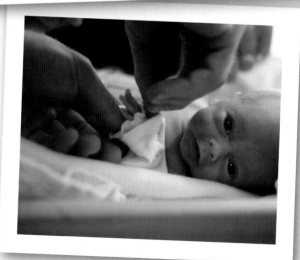

Kathryn Langford

SHOW THE
Emotion

Think of meaningful feelings or concepts you'd like to illustrate with your photo: innocence, newness, fragility, joy, blessings.

SHOTS TO TRY:

Baby in dad's arms ✱ Asleep over mom or dad's shoulder ✱ Curled up in her crib on her tummy ✱ Close-ups of tiny fingers and toes ✱ Baby naked or in a diaper ✱ Baby all in white or swaddled in a blanket with just the face showing ✱ In hospital bassinet ✱ Hospital nursery environment ✱ Funny newborn facial expressions ✱ Nursing ✱ Sleeping ✱ Crying ✱ Hat on/off ✱ Shots taken above looking down and at eye level ✱ Asleep on mom or dad ✱ Siblings or relatives holding the new baby

Kathryn Langford

75

Babies

"Everybody loves a baby
that's why I'm in love with you."
— Jackson, Kahn &
Van Alstyne, "Pretty Baby"

In America, we use words like "sweet, cute and darling" to describe our babies. The Australians call them "gorgeous." And gorgeous they are, with creamy skin and chubby legs and arms; it's hard to not want to squeeze, kiss and cuddle them every chance you get. Babies at the pre-walking age are great photographic subjects because they are captive models!

Creative Challenge

Show surroundings Try introducing the baby's surroundings into your shots. Get parts and pieces of your house or her room in the background, making for a much more meaningful memory of that time in her life.

Introduce a sense of scale Highlight how small the baby is in this big world. Sit the baby in an oversized chair or have him stand up to a windowsill, highlighting his tiny size.

Get in close Those eyes, eyelashes and sweet little cheeks and lips all look wonderful up close and personal. Zoom all the way in or try a macro lens to get the close-ups of that sweet face. Remember to watch for the little flakes of skin around the nose and in the corners of the mouths when photographing babies.

Explore your viewpoint Try the same shot from different viewpoints and cropping. The resulting images can be used to create a triptych (a series of three images) in a frame commonly known as a storyboard. Storyboards provide a contemporary, museumlike feel and prove the theory of the sum being greater than the parts. Storyboards often give an overall feel or representation of one child, one day, one moment in time better than a single image can.

SHOW THE
Emotion

Think of meaningful descriptive terms you can illustrate with your photo: chubby, gorgeous, messy, sweet, soft, slobbery, sleepy.

SHOTS TO TRY:

*Get down low and take a shot of the baby crawling away from you * Take a shot from inside the baby's crib looking out (her view of her room) * First foods * Close-up of the first tooth * Drool on the lips * Hairstyles * Sleeping * Emotions * Reaching for toys * Favorite blankie * Smiles and giggles * Close-ups of eyes and chubby fists/feet * Bathtime * In stroller/car seat * Pulling up in their crib*

Janelle Smith

Amanda Keeys

77

Toddlers

With their brand-new bodies and tons of attitude, toddlers are ready to take the world by storm. Everything is new; everything is an adventure. They are driven to try it all out by climbing, touching or tasting the world around them. The personalities begin to emerge in a big way as they tell you, "No!" It's always a bit amazing to be told off by a two-and-a-half-year-old who has mastered the attitude but can't quite manage the potty training! Make it a priority to capture the wonder and the attitude in your toddler's world.

Creative Challenge

See the parts of the whole Very often, the most meaningful shots are not the ones taken with the child looking into the camera or posing with a cheesy grin. Instead, think about the characteristics that are most appealing about this age. The dimpled hands and soft cheeks, the roundness of their features and how cute they are.

Capture the calm Because toddlers always seem to be in motion, it's a trick to try and capture a few shots of them in repose. Try photographing your toddler while she's asleep or concentrating intensely on something else. Hand her your cell phone and move in close for the face shot.

Make a noise While your toddler is concentrating, make a sound to get him to look up. You can capture beautiful expressions this way.

Be quick The only way to capture the nonstop action of a toddler is a fast shutter speed and quick feet. Chase after her and get the shot.

Get on their level Don't forget to get down on the toddlers' level to avoid the big-head-little-feet syndrome created by aiming your camera down at kids.

Show favorites Capture a few shots that illustrate your child's favorites at this stage. Think of favorite foods or a special blankie or toy.

"There are no little things. 'Little things' are the hinges of the universe."
— Fanny Fern

Amanda Keeys

Barb Uil

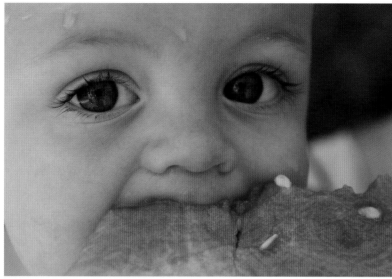

Janelle Smith

SHOW THE
Emotion

Illustrate meaningful descriptive terms with your photo: chubby, gorgeous, messy, sweet, soft, slobbery, sleepy, sassy, naughty, curious, delighted, mischievous.

SHOTS TO TRY:

Their toys ✳ Their favorite blankie or lovey ✳ If they are still sucking the pacifier, include it ✳ The fat bottle-belly hanging over the diaper ✳ The dimpled hands and feet ✳ Interacting with other babies ✳ The cute little fingers ✳ picking up food or pushing buttons on toys ✳ First spoon ✳ Messy face ✳ Outdoors in the water, sand or grass ✳ Cute details on their clothing ✳ First shoes ✳ Fat rolls on arms and legs ✳ With the family ✳ Climbing ✳ Playing in cupboards ✳ Sleeping ✳ Tantrums ✳ Story time ✳ Potty training ✳ Snuggles ✳ Imitating others ✳ Kissing parents/siblings ✳ Eating treats, lollipops and ice cream ✳ Birthday celebrations

Creative Challenge

Capture the everyday The everyday activities of a toddler may seem insignificant today, but years from now, these funny little quirks and bursts of personality, if captured, will be priceless memories. Think about the things that your toddler does that just crack you up.

Show off the tricks What are the "tricks" you make her show off for Grandma? How can you best capture her amazing enthusiasm for life? Run your toddler through her paces of favorite nursery rhymes or "What does a doggie say?" for some of the cutest expressions you'll ever see.

Document affection Toddlers love to get snuggly, kissy and huggy with those they love and trust. Capturing these endearing moments is a must.

"I want the wide hugs and the exclamations of delight."
– Sabrina Ward Harrison

Kathryn Langford

Kathryn Langford

SHOW THE
Emotion

Think of terms of toddlerhood you'd like to illustrate with your photo: fearless, shy, finicky, silly, personality, "No!"

SHOTS TO TRY:

"Fly on the wall" shots where the child is unaware of you ✽ *Responses to questions ("Where's the cow?")—toddlers often seriously consider these with the cutest expressions* ✽ *Playtime* ✽ *Puzzles* ✽ *Napping in interesting places* ✽ *Bubble bath* ✽ *Playing with the hose* ✽ *Taking penny pony rides* ✽ *Pushing or pulling things much larger than they are* ✽ *Purses or carriers* ✽ *Hairstyles* ✽ *Games with family* ✽ *Kicking a ball* ✽ *Running* ✽ *Wearing her mom or dad's shoes* ✽ *Dancing to music*

PHOTO ART
Show Off Your Baby

If you remember to take your camera with you, even an ordinary drive can result in art for your home. A family drive down the Florida coast was interrupted when two-year-old Gracie shrieked in delight at seeing the beach. Although a swim wasn't in the plans, this little girl immediately stripped down to her undies and made a break for the water with her beloved "Poppa" not far behind. Luckily, her grandma had remembered the camera and was able to capture the carefree toddler and her adoring grandfather enjoying a moment together in the sun and sand. The resulting photos were collaged together in Photoshop and made into a poster for Gracie's bedroom as a memento of their day together.

Donna Smylie

82

STEP-BY-STEP

① Convert images to black and white in Photoshop.

② Create a blank document with a black background to the size of your choice (in this case the size was 30" x 40" [76cm x 102cm]).

③ From the View menu select Show›Grid to act as a guideline for placing your photos.

④ Once you have placed your photos and flattened the document you can upload it to your favorite lab and have it mounted (in this case on black foamcore).

Variations

- *Don't limit yourself to the standard 4" x 6" (10cm x 15cm) or 5" x 7" (13cm x 18cm) prints from your local lab. Try having a favorite image enlarged to poster size for your child's room or as a gift to a friend.*
- *As long as the poster is properly mounted on foamcore of polystyrene, framing is optional.*

Preschool

Don't be afraid to capture the mismatched ensemble, the messiness of it all. Years ago, we had a mother bring her well-scrubbed, perfectly coiffed, preschool-aged girls to have their photos taken. Later, when she came to pick up her proofs, girls in tow, the girls had on overalls with tutus over the top, sunglasses, headphones and the most fabulous array of costume jewelry ever seen on a preschooler. Their ponytails were askew and their faces a bit dirty— your basic photographer's dream. We said to the mom, "Why didn't you bring them like this?" Her response was, "Oh, they look like this all the time." And that would be the whole point. Yes, they might look like this all the time *now*. But now doesn't last forever. They won't still be dressing like this at eight or ten. Preschoolers make for some of the best photographic subjects. You don't have to coach them. They aren't one bit self-conscious; just let them do their thing and be ready to shoot.

Creative Challenge

Show the baby Capture the parts that show the baby still underneath all that dress up. Focus on the chubby legs, cheeks and elbows and the cute, dimpled hands to tell the story of a baby on the move.

Show just a part of the whole This allows our imagination to fill in the rest of the scene. Zoom in close and capture the bits and pieces that tell a larger story. That little hip out to the side makes for a perfect "s" curve that keeps your interest on the photo. There's no directing a toddler, so it's just luck if you can get it!

Use dreamy filters or actions Photoshop effects can add an otherworldly feel to your little princess's images. Do a Google search for Photoshop Actions and you'll see tons of Web sites with free Photoshop actions for you to try. The photo of the little girl in the pink dress on the opposite page was enhanced using the Midnight Sepia action.

84

Ruth Giauque

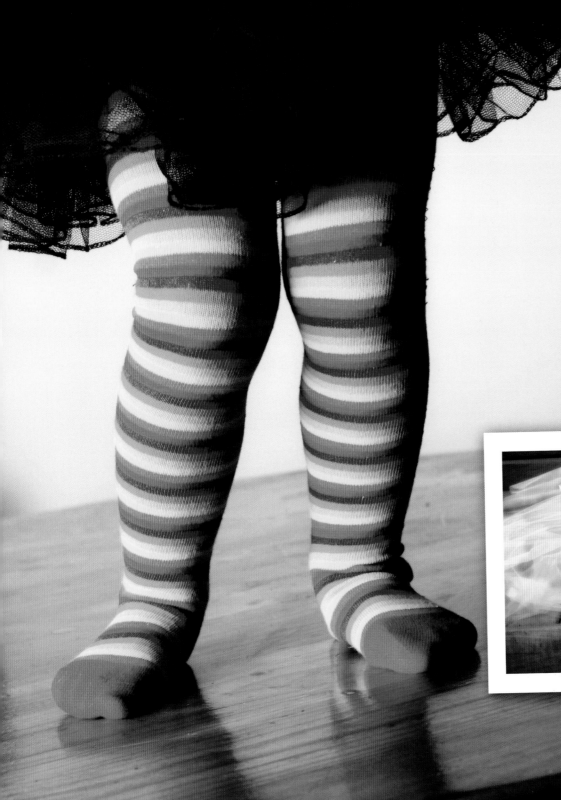

SHOW THE
Emotion

Think of meaningful feelings and concepts you'd like to illustrate with your photo: imagination, pretend, dreams, experimentation, curiosity, "Mine!"

SHOTS TO TRY:

Dressing themselves ❋ Profiles of the still-chubby cheeks ❋ Close-ups of the mismatched shoes/outfits ❋ A favorite pet (even if it's his grandpa) ❋ The self-inflicted haircut ❋ The inventive thumbsucker ❋ Naptime ❋ Messes they've made ❋ Dressing themselves ❋ The potty training efforts

Amanda Keeys

85

If you want the best images of your preschooler, remember this simple advice: Shoot first; discipline later. Document the trouble they get into as it's happening, that way you'll have photos to go with the hair-raising tales. Also, children between the ages of three and five become more involved in the world outside the home with preschool and lessons breaking up their day. Make it a point to take your camera with you to document their activities.

Creative Challenge

Chronicle "a day in the life of ..." Have you considered spending one day, camera in hand, documenting the life of your preschooler? Mentally pull yourself out of your daily routine and try to see it as an outsider would. If an anthropologist came to your home for a day, what would she document about your child's living, eating and behavior patterns?

Push your boundaries Rather than getting the same old shot of your child on the swing, why not try something different? Is the light harsh enough to get a good shadow? Wait for the moment when he is outlined in the frame and take your shot.

Capture quirks Does your child stick out his tongue or furrow his brow when he is deep in concentration? Using a long, or telephoto, lens allows you to be out of the way and capture these moments without anyone knowing you were there.

Simplify the image Rather than settling for the far-off shots of your child at his swim lesson, simplify the image by zooming in and documenting his valiant attempts to stay afloat. Using the rule of thirds, put him off center for a more interesting shot.

Document favorites Set yourself the task of a photo essay called "Favorites at Five" (or whatever age your child is).

SHOW THE
Emotion

Think of meaningful feelings and concepts you'd like to illustrate with your photo: possiblity, energy, adventure, disaster, enthusiasm, unstoppable, fearless.

SHOTS TO TRY:

Just before waking up ✻ *Waking up* ✻ *Being tickled* ✻ *Jumping on the bed* ✻ *Breakfast time* ✻ *Playing at the park* ✻ *Playing* ✻ *Trying new things* ✻ *Activities* ✻ *Naptime* ✻ *Lessons* ✻ *Dad getting home from work* ✻ *Carpooling with all the kids in the backseat* ✻ *Bath and bedtime routines*

Preschool Girls

If you're a parent of a little girl, it might not have escaped your notice as to who's the boss in your house. More mature than boys their same age (and even their older brothers) preschool-aged girls can run rings around the boys in the household (especially their dads!). The amount of drama and attitude generated by a single girl can make for some of the best shots you'll ever get.

Creative Challenge

Capture the innocence Don't be afraid to show the teeth falling out and the spaces in between. It's all part of being this age.

Show the dichotomy of her personality Document the girlie-girl princess and then contrast that with the wild-child moments.

Capture her sense of style and personality Shoot a photo essay with a combination of action and more posed shots. Remember not to be so concerned with the technical aspects of photography that you forget to capture the emotion that is happening before your eyes.

88

Amanda Keeys

SHOW THE
Emotion

Think of meaningful feelings and descriptive terms you'd like to illustrate with your photo: sweet, sassy, bossy, dramatic, princess, high maintenance, loving, gentle.

SHOTS TO TRY:

Hands on hips ✳ Bossing siblings around ✳ With dolls or favorite toys ✳ Daddy's girl ✳ The dirty look during the timeout ✳ Messy and dirty ✳ A photo essay of favorites ✳ The perfect princess ✳ The Barbie fest ✳ Playing with pals ✳ Tomboy ✳ Wearing fifteen outfits in one day ✳ Tea party

Amanda Keeys

Kathryn Langford

89

Preschool Boys

In motion from morning 'til night, preschool boys are bundles of energy. Walking doesn't really happen at this age; they run everywhere, jump from high places and create swords and all manner of weapons from the unlikeliest of materials.

Creative Challenge

Keep the camera ready No matter how tough they think they are, we know they are just marshmallows at heart. There is a sweet, endearing innocence in a preschool boy. Capture it by keeping your camera by your side.

Keep your eye on the ball Have your son hold a favorite toy away from him and using a short depth of field, focus on the ball and allow him to go out of focus. The try the opposite and see which one you like better.

Go toward the light Take advantage of window light to capture the wild boy in his native environment: his room.

Janelle Smith

Janelle Smith

Janelle Smith

SHOW THE
Emotion

Think of meaningful feelings and concepts you'd like to illustrate with your photo: roughness, messiness, activity, dirtiness, mischief, adventure.

SHOTS TO TRY:

The messy room ✱ Momma's boy ✱ Favorite toys ✱ A day at the park jungle gym, swings, etc. ✱ Riding his trike, bike, vehicle of the moment ✱ Superhero in training ✱ The tree house or fort ✱ His inventions ✱ The Legos or other structures ✱ Daily adventures ✱ Neighborhood highjinks ✱ Games of hide and seek with friends and/ or siblings

Elementary School

Entering school is most children's first step into the wide world beyond home. In school all day, they learn to work and play with others, and friends become vital to their ever-expanding social life. Hobbies and interests begin to emerge as they are enrolled in lessons and try out new activities on their own. School-aged children are literally learning something new every day. It's an exciting time of learning and growth that is a joy to capture.

Creative Challenge

School portraits You know those really bad school photos that come home every year, and you just have to buy them because it's your kid? Why not designate yourself as the photographer for your child at the beginning of each school year and get the shots you really want, the ones that actually show off the personality of your child? To document the new fall fashions try a more pulled-back shot taking in the whole child, outfit, attitude and all.

Include pets For a different take on the typical kid-with-pet shot, let the family pet do his own thing and see what happens!

Get rid of the background Focus on the action by using a short depth of field to blur the background.

Best friends There is no relationship so passionate as that of grade-school girls. Friends one minute, bitterest of enemies the next. Get them talking and capture the happy moments.

Amanda Keeys

Amanda Keeys

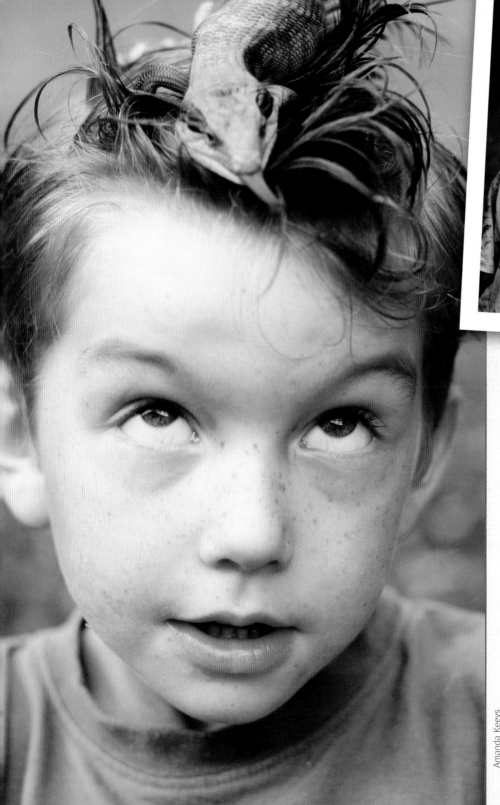

Amanda Keeys

Amanda Keeys

SHOW THE
Emotion

Think of meaningful concepts you'd like to illustrate with your photo: accomplishment, enthusiasm, friendship, creativity, learning, potential, growth.

SHOTS TO TRY:

Toothless grins ✱ Back-to-school fashion statement ✱ Holes in their jeans ✱ Science projects ✱ Jeans getting too short ✱ First report card ✱ Giggling with their friends ✱ Field trips ✱ Getting on the bus ✱ The backpack and school gear ✱ On the playground ✱ The stack of books ✱ In their classroom—with a favorite teacher ✱ Their shoes ✱ Playing sports—on the bench or on the field ✱ Creativity—be it rock houses, fingerpaintings or the fort in the living room ✱ Backstage at their latest performance/recital ✱ Doing chores ✱ In the neighborhood, on bikes, with friends ✱ Achievements—trophies and ribbons

93

Junior High

"Be yourself.
No one can ever tell you
you're doing it wrong."
— James Leo Herlihy

Adolescence is termed the "awkward stage" for a reason. Most children at this age have features and bodies they haven't quite grown into yet. Add to that the complexion challenges, the need for braces and sometimes glasses, and we are left with a surly kid who isn't very camera friendly. And we won't even get started on the mood swings and attitude. Taking photos of children at this stage, while not easy, can encourage them to loosen up a bit with the added benefit of giving their self esteem a boost.

Creative Challenge

Take it in stride Photographing adolescents is much like trying to climb a cactus. They can be a bit prickly and hard to get on with. Even though they think they know it all, adolescents still need a loving and affectionate shoulder to lean on. As you're shooting the photos, joke with them and let them know how beautiful or tough they look and watch the façade melt away.

Janelle Smith

94

Audrey Woulard

SHOW THE
Emotion

Think of meaningful descriptive terms you'd like to illustrate with your photo: awkward, self-conscious, prickly yet sweet, insecure, daring, tough yet vulnerable.

SHOTS TO TRY:

"Tin grin" after the braces are put on ✳ Set up a "photo shoot" with their friends ✳ On their skateboard or bike ✳ Glasses or contacts ✳ Clothes, clothes, clothes ✳ Dressed up or down ✳ Church activities ✳ Extracurricular activities ✳ Friends ✳ Video games and other hobbies and obsessions ✳ Favorite activities ✳ Muscles ✳ Studying ✳ Eating ✳ Doing hair ✳ Applying makeup

Audrey Woulard

95

High School

"I am not afraid.
I was born to do this."
— Joan of Arc

Never more beautiful and yet still insecure about how they look and where they fit into the grand scheme of their lives, high-school-aged teens talk like adults, think they should be treated like adults but sometimes act just like kids. The girls want to be fashion models, and the boys are looking for the NBA contracts in the mail. The majority of their time is spent beyond home now as they are tied up in school activities and friends. They get their first job and find out the world's not fair; they get their first serious boy- or girlfriend and get their hearts broken. Full of promise for the future and energy for the present, kids in their late teens are fun to photograph.

Creative Challenge

Capture the bedroom Using the widest setting on your zoom lens, get a shot of your teen's entire room (and don't make her clean it first, Mom!). Years from now, every bit of paper on that floor will bring back a memory for her.
Find some decent light Rather than backing your prom-goers up against the front door and flashing them to death, try taking them outside for some natural light.

SHOW THE
Emotion

Think of meaningful feelings and concepts you'd like to illustrate with your photo: independence, style, confidence, fun, maturity, immaturity, responsibility.

SHOTS TO TRY:

Prom night ✻ *Before the big date* ✻ *Fashion shoot—look at magazines for posing and location ideas* ✻ *On the computer* ✻ *Listening to the iPod* ✻ *On the cell phone* ✻ *Hanging out with friends* ✻ *Driving* ✻ *After the braces come off* ✻ *Their latest passions and fashions* ✻ *Watching TV* ✻ *Playing sports* ✻ *Reading teen magazines* ✻ *Studying* ✻ *First paycheck* ✻ *Shaving* ✻ *Boyfriends/girlfriends*

PHOTO ART
Show Off Your Kids

When you just can't decide which photo to use, use them all! Cover the front of your album with photos from your latest shoot and give the whole project a distressed feel using sandpaper and funky, retro embellishments. Make one for each child photographed and, while you're at it, you might as well do one for the grandparents, too!

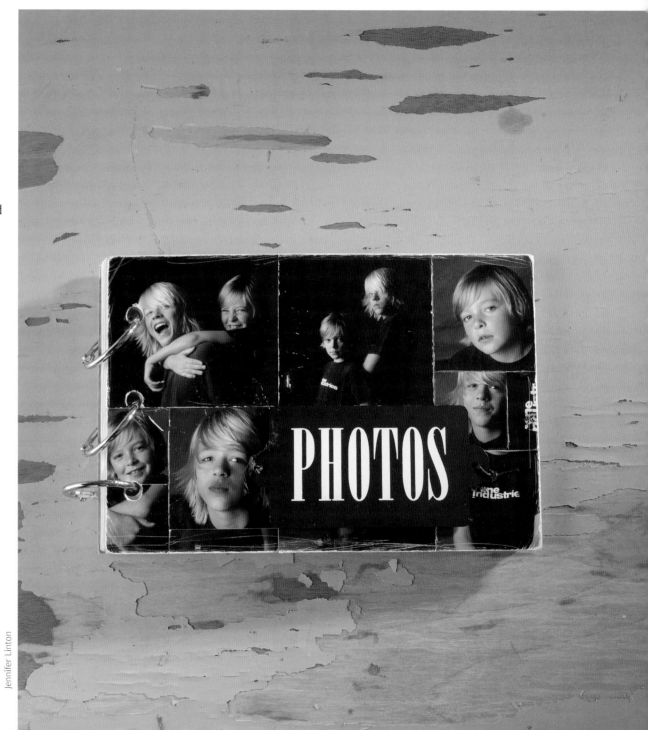

Jennifer Linton

① Purchase or make a board-covered album using acid-free book board, cardstock and binder rings. (Our album and embellishments are by 7gypsies.)

② Cut photos into sizes that will complete a pleasing photo collage for the cover of your book.

③ Using fine sandpaper, sand the edges of the photos to give a funky, worn look to the cover then adhere them to the cover of your book.

④ Use the index print that comes with your photos as strips to decorate a page.

Variations

✗ Buy a ready-made blank board book and use full-size images trimmed at the edges of the board pages to create your own custom board book featuring your child.

✗ Let your kids get in on the act. Get duplicate prints of the photos and let them make their own book.

99

Young Adults

Young adulthood is a time of risk and discovery. From the excitement of college life to the "real world" scariness of new graduates competing in the real job market, the world is their oyster, all they have to do is figure out who they are and what they want to do with the rest of their lives. No pressure.

Creative Challenge

Take a self-portrait Self-portraits are a revealing look at how we see ourselves. Young adulthood is an introspective time when we try to figure ourselves out; a good time to try a self-portrait. Make it a habit, take a self-portrait once a year, every year. Hold your camera at arm's length and shoot away. You'll make lots of blurry images but one or two will come out. Using a tripod will give you the best results. Just press the timer and run quick. Move in closer with a zoom lens and pick up the parts that are unique to you. Maybe it's those piano fingers that are so admired; the new pedicure or perhaps you consider your eyes your best asset. Focus on what's unique about you, even if it's not pretty. Don't give up too soon. Keep shooting until you get a photo that captures the real you.

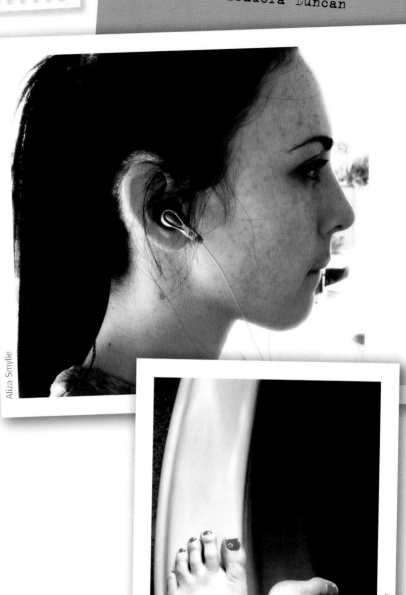

Aliza Smylie

Aliza Smylie

100

Aliza Smylie

Aliza Smylie

SHOW THE
Emotion

Think of meaningful feelings, concepts and milestones you'd like to illustrate with your photo: leaving home, experimentation, freedom, happiness, depression, pride, hilarity.

SHOTS TO TRY:

Artifacts of life at this stage * Stack of textbooks * Spring break and other trips * Dorm room * Roommates * Car (exterior/interior) (or other modes of transportation) * Road trips * Workplace * Friends * Fashion trends * Shoes * Hairstyles * Music * Dancing * Parties * Concerts

101

Couples

Was it love at first sight, or were they friends first? Where did they meet? When did they first know that there was a spark? It seems like a miracle when the right connection is made, when two people understand each other so well...they totally "get" each other in every way. Finding the love of your life doesn't happen everyday, so when it does, capture the passion and happiness in as many ways as you can. Just think, when they're celebrating their fiftieth wedding anniversary, how glad they'll be for the fabulous photos of when they were young and newly in love.

Creative Challenge

Walking away One of the nicest shots to get is the couple walking down a path or road, hand in hand, together. It gives a universal feel of happily ever after.

Try a triptych Set yourself an assignment of a photo essay for the couple. Using the triptych layout, shoot images for a storyboard of love.

Capture the reaction Tell him to whisper sweet nothings in her ear and then shoot her reactions to whatever he does. Watch for the "in-betweens"—the things that happen in-between the more posed shots you are trying.

Ruth Giauque

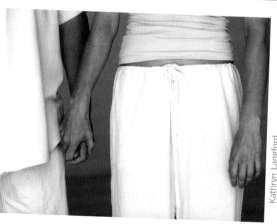
Kathryn Langford

102

SHOW THE
Emotion

Think of meaningful feelings and concepts you'd like to illustrate: adoration, passion, beginning, future, love, soul mates, always.

SHOTS TO TRY:

Eating at a favorite restaurant ✱ *Hands in each other's pockets* ✱
Grocery shopping together ✱ *Favorite activities* ✱ *Favorite places*
✱ *Just their hands together* ✱ *Walking away* ✱ *Running forward* ✱
Piggy back ✱ *Being silly* ✱ *Kissing* ✱ *Hugging* ✱ *Laughing*

Austin Smylie

Kathryn Langford

103

Weddings

You won't see today's wedding photographer spending hours on end setting up group after group of relatives to photograph. More likely, she'll be sneaking up behind the bride putting on her veil or the flower girls sharing secrets. The photojournalistic trend in wedding photography has raised the bar for all portrait photography by placing a premium on capturing emotion and meaning during one of life's most important rituals.

Creative Challenge

Group shots with the relatives These are still and will always be a must-have for most brides, but they don't have to look like a police line-up. Move in closer and take the photo as a three-quarter shot, cropping off the legs and feet of the group and focusing more on their faces.

Forget the flash Most churches won't allow you to use them during the ceremony, anyway. If you're shooting indoors and there are some good windows around, take advantage of the light available and crank the ISO setting on your camera up to 1600 or higher (or use equivalent speed film). Your images will be grainier than if you used flash but great light with grain is preferable to flash without.

Quiet moments Take the time to get a photo of the mother-of–the-bride and the bride during a quiet moment together and also the bride with her father. In a very real way, they are giving their daughter away today.

Getting ready One of the most popular parts of the wedding day has become the "before" photos of the bride and her maids getting ready. Don't forget the flowergirls!

104

Janelle Smith

SHOW THE
Emotion

Think of meaningful feelings and concepts you'd like to illustrate with your photo: romance, fairy tale, forever, happily ever after, family, "I Do," magic, promises.

SHOTS TO TRY:

The groom seeing the bride in her dress ✱ *The rings* ✱ *Bridesmaids at the beauty shop* ✱ *Parents of the bride and/or groom wiping away tears* ✱ *Bride getting ready* ✱ *Dancing with the parents* ✱ *"Parts" of the wedding: flowers, cake, favors, etc.* ✱ *The church* ✱ *The car or carriage* ✱ *Interactions between the guests* ✱ *First moments as husband and wife* ✱ *Arrival and departure of bride and groom* ✱ *First dance as husband and wife*

PHOTO ART
Show Off the Couple

Celebrate the beginning of a new family by repurposing relics from your family's past. In this project a collection of old frames and junk was gathered to create a focal point for a stairway. You probably have lots of things hanging around your house that would be perfect for your own display. For this couple, we used images from their engagement photo shoot plus gifts they received for their wedding and some old frames and salvage items culled from the garages of family members.

Allison Tyler Jones

STEP-BY-STEP

① Find or have made a very large frame to act as the outside boundary of your display.

② With a pencil, mark the interior measurement of the frame directly onto the wall.

③ Paint directly on the wall inside the markings using a contrasting paint color.
Variation: If you would rather not paint directly on your wall, you can have a piece of homosote board (available at home improvement stores) cut to size and cover it with the fabric of your choice and mount it inside the frame—then hang each item directly onto the homosote board.

④ Lay the large frame on the floor and position your items inside to get an idea of a pleasing layout for your display. Once you have the basic layout, snap a photo or make a sketch to remind you of the positioning and you are ready to hang.

Variations

✴ Try using salvage items such as old doorknobs, hinges, corbels, letters from old signs or pieces of tin from old buildings or old frames, damaged or not, that can be used as-is or repainted.

✴ Add vintage ribbons, lace or old costume jewelry for a more feminine feel.

✴ This project also would be a great way to display a child's certificates, trophies and other evidences of his accomplishments.

Family Photojournalist

There is no photographer you could hire who knows your family as well as you do. As the photojournalist for your family, you have unparalleled access to your subject matter plus the emotional connection to them that allows you to get the shots that capture the personalities in your family and relationships between them. Environmental portraits include the surroundings as part of the subject of the photo. Consider areas in the home that are significant for the family such as the kitchen counter or table where everyone hangs out. Be on the lookout for particular artwork or musical instruments that can add meaning and an element of storytelling to your next family portrait.

Barb Uil

Creative Challenge

Show your family by the foot Try an extreme horizontal panoramic shot of your family. Get everyone's feet or just everyone's faces. Line 'em up and shoot!

Celebrate your mom and dad Remember that they started this whole thing in the first place. Don't forget to snap one or two of just them together.

Show relationships Focusing on one child and letting the rest of the family act as background is a great storytelling technique for a family portrait.

Study the home Stairways provide a perfect setup for photographing siblings. Find a set of steps or a stairway with decent lighting and snap away. Accept the challenge to find great places in and around the home. Look for good light and interesting furniture or architectural features that will add interest and meaning to the image.

Barb Uil

SHOW THE
Emotion

Think of meaningful feelings and concepts you'd like to illustrate with your photo: comfort, connection, togetherness, home, haven, real life.

SHOTS TO TRY:

Hanging out ✴ Celebrations ✴ Family favorites ✴ The family bed ✴ Our house ✴ Front or back porch ✴ Bedrooms ✴ Swimming pool ✴ Dinner table ✴ Playing games ✴ Outdoor sports ✴ The family car ✴ Tickle time

Audrey Woulard

109

Family Groups

The hardest shot in the world to get right is the family group. In short, it's a recipe for disaster. The stress that mothers go through to make the family picture a reality could put anyone on a psychiatrist's couch. They shop for weeks for the clothes, make sure all the haircuts happen and threaten everyone within an inch of his life if he gets dirty on the way to the shoot. Then there's the fathers. It may not have escaped your notice that the most difficult person in each family group to keep happy is not the two-year-old; more often, it's dear old dad. You want an image that conveys the loving bond between the family members, and everyone is stressed out and over it before it's even begun. Is it any wonder we often settle for a police line-up of the parties involved just to be done with it? Next time around, start with the feeling you'd like to convey first. Determine what the culture of this family is. Are they formal and more restrained or more playful and carefree? Consider locations and activities that will work with the family style rather than trying to make them fit into a situation that just doesn't work for them.

Creative Challenge

Unify the group Loosen things up a bit by providing an activity for everyone to participate in or by selecting a unifying element, like dad's antique car or the local park, as a background for the shot.

Emphasize with focus Break the rule that says everyone in the photo has to be in focus. Put the kids up front and let the parents blur out in the background.

Emphasize with silhouettes Set your camera's exposure for the strong backlighting to get a silhouette effect of a specific family group with a universal appeal.

Audrey Woulard

SHOW THE
Emotion

Think of the meaning you'd like your photo to represent: teamwork, love, quality time, connections, closeness, fun.

SHOTS TO TRY:

Walking hand in hand toward and away from the camera ✻ Kids running toward the camera with parents in the background ✻ Silhouette of family against bright background ✻ Kids tackling dad ✻ Dogpile of kids ✻ The girls with their mom ✻ The boys with their dad ✻ The girls with their dad ✻ The boys with their mom ✻ Kids chasing the dog

Siblings

Corralling the entire family for a group shot is rewarding, but difficult. There are so many personalities, it's hard to capture the intricacies. With brothers and sisters, you'll find power struggles, endearing protectiveness, competition, camaraderie. One minute it's "all for one and one for all." The next, it's class warfare. Before you begin shooting, size up the relationships. Who gets along with who, and where are the rivalries? Capture these dichotomies and capture some of the most compelling images you'll ever take.

Creative Challenge

Get real If your kids are couch potatoes some of the time (and whose aren't?), capture those television moments.

Provoke a response You can capture some fantastic expressions just by asking silly questions ("Who's the naughtiest?") that will make them look at each other in a spontaneous way. Or try, "Give each other a big kiss!" Don't worry about the kiss being "the shot"—what happens before and after the kiss is often the best stuff.

Keep shooting Even when things get ugly, stay calm and keep snapping. It's all part of the real life of siblings. While you don't want situations to escalate into arm punches and hair pulling, keep a lighthearted attitude that encourages the rivalry.

> "I don't know how people learn to live in the world if they haven't had siblings."
> — Anna Quindlen

Barb Uil

Kathryn Langford

SHOW THE
Emotion

Think of the meaningful feelings and concepts you'd like to illustrate with your photo: love, hate, camaraderie, competition, nature, rivalry, bossiness, silliness, roughness, gentility, nurturing.

SHOTS TO TRY:

Brothers ✱ Older kids with the younger ✱ Sisters ✱ Piggyback rides ✱ Individual siblings ✱ Facing each other nose to nose ✱ Comparing heights back to back ✱ Bear hugs ✱ Playing ✱ Muscle competition ✱ Fighting ✱ Bunk beds or sharing a bedroom ✱ Laughing ✱ Pick your favorite toy/prop ✱ Crying ✱ Kisses/wiping off the kisses ✱ Follow along on a game of hide-and-seek or tag ✱ Sharing secrets ✱ Dogpile

113

Family Gatherings

"One cannot have too
large a party."
— Jane Austen

Holidays, birthday parties and family reunions are a time to reflect on the years that have flown by, to connect with loved ones we don't see often and celebrate the rituals that define our lives. Family gatherings are also an excellent time to snap a few shots of the family, both immediate and extended. Make time to do a little clandestine photo shoot of your sibling's children, favorite cousins together, grandparents with all the grandkids. Print up the photos without anyone knowing, and you've got Christmas gifts that will have them searching for a hankie.

Creative Challenge

Take a step back Too often we are in the thick of things when we just need to pull back a bit and get an outsider's view of our events and rituals. Find a vantage point a bit further away than you'd normally shoot and see what results.

Organize the group Corral everyone out on the back porch for an impromptu group shot with great lighting. Don't worry if the toddlers won't stay put, using the group as a background for a child in the foreground is a fresh take on the typical "line-up."

Capture interaction Watch for those moments when the cousins start the cannonball competition or when Grandpa and his granddaughter team up to beat Dad in a game of Yahtzee. Get Grandma and her daughters cooking in the kitchen and sharing the latest gossip.

Barb Uil

SHOW THE
Emotion

Think of meaningful feelings and concepts you'd like to illustrate with your photo: celebration, multiple generations, family, togetherness, love, discovery, communication.

SHOTS TO TRY:

Favorite aunts and uncles ✽ Family meetings and reunions ✽ The cousins ✽ Singing ✽ Grandparents ✽ Performing ✽ New babies ✽ Eating ✽ In the kitchen ✽ Generations ✽ Traditions ✽ Laughing ✽ Quiet times ✽ Kids asleep ✽ Grandpa asleep

Barb Uil

115

Family Vacations

A family vacation is a time where dad can relax, mom doesn't worry about cleaning up the house and the kids get a break from schoolwork and chores. The distractions of everyday life fade away, freeing everyone to get to know each other in a different way. Traveling through a strange land invites camaraderie among the band of family travelers as they trudge through museums during the day and play card games late into the night. No matter where you're headed, the family vacation allows for lots of uninterrupted, quality family time. Take the opportunity to put a spin on your normal travel pics. Document the highlights, for sure, but don't forget to get a picture of that fleabag motel room you got stuck with, or dad with his head under the hood of the RV that just broke down. It's all part of the journey that is the family vacation.

Creative Challenge

Worm's-eye view If you want a gorgeous shot of a monument, buy the postcard. If you want an interesting shot of someone in your family in front of a monument, change your viewpoint to make the person larger in the frame with the monument as background. Get down low and shoot up at your subject and the monument, making the person appear larger in the frame.

Real-world view Try this the next time you take a shot of an activity. Position yourself where you have part of the subject close to you in the frame and another part further away. This makes for a much more interesting shot because this is more how we experience our world.

Austin Smylie

116

Barb Uil

SHOW THE
Emotion

Think of meaningful feelings and concepts you'd like to illustrate with your photo: wanderlust, adventure, postcards, tourists, jet lag, scenery, companionship, new horizons, vagabonds, thrill seekers.

SHOTS TO TRY:

The sights ✱ Shopping ✱ Doorways and windows ✱ The food ✱ New experiences ✱ Abstract pieces of famous monuments ✱ The music ✱ Local entertainment ✱ The locals ✱ Silliness ✱ The architecture ✱ Local hot spots ✱ The hotel/motel ✱ The locals ✱ The transportation ✱ The tour guide ✱ Your favorite doorman/taxi driver/maid, etc. ✱ Souvenir shopping ✱ Signs and directions (in all languages) ✱ Getting lost ✱ Hiking the trail

Austin Smylie

117

Generations

Isn't it funny how the woman that raised you, spanked your fanny and grounded you when you were bad is the same person making lame excuses for your child's naughty behavior? A match made in heaven, the grandparent-grandchild relationship is a tender bond with fierce loyalties on both sides and woe to the parent who tries to get in the middle of it! Grandparents are fabulous to photograph because, for the most part, they've given up on being fashion-model self-conscious and are more comfortable with who they are. That and the fact that they are absolutely crazy about their grandkids makes for a dream photo shoot. So, don't wait until a grandparent is sick or ailing to take photos of them with your children. Make the effort to get out the camera at every opportunity.

Creative Challenge

Capture the interaction Since the grandparent's focus is always on the grandchild, take your cue and focus on the child using the grandparent as a "background" of sorts. Capture the interaction and the love between them.

Be a little bit sneaky Strap on a long lens and capture grandparents and their grandchildren spending time together without them ever even knowing you were there.

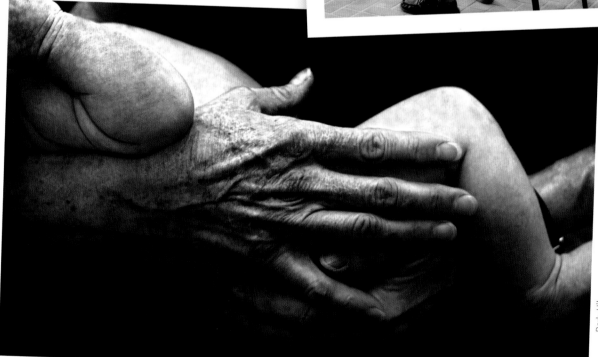

Barb Uil

Amanda Keeys

SHOW THE
Emotion

Think of meaningful feelings and concepts you'd like to illustrate with your photo: nurturing, gentle strength, age and wisdom, youth and exuberance, teaching, unconditional love, support, adoration.

SHOTS TO TRY:

Hands, old and young ✻ Sharing hobbies ✻ Reading stories ✻ Family recipes or meals ✻ Ticklefest with grandpa ✻ Hugs and kisses ✻ Playing games, jigsaw puzzles ✻ Helping grandma/grandpa ✻ Taking walks ✻ Sitting on the porch ✻ In the grandparents' environment

Kathryn Langford

119

Images for Posterity

What do you want your grandchildren to know about you? What do you wish you knew about your great-grandparents? What pictures do you wish had been taken of those who have gone before you? Taking photos with future generations in mind can add a timeless style to your work. Rather than Grandpa Jones at his eightieth birthday party, you might take a photo that says, "gentle strength." Capture the experience and wisdom as well as that nineteen-year-old who still lives inside of us all.

Creative Challenge

Use sidelighting for texture Besides the eyes, the hands are the most expressive and unique parts of a human being. The hands of an older person tell a story all their own. Take advantage of the side lighting from a window or door to capture every bit of texture.

Photograph age and life endurance If you are lucky enough to have a parent or grandparent who is willing to share the battle scars that life has dealt them, rise to the challenge and do your best work.

Celebrate the wisdom Don't let your mother or grandmother talk you out of taking her photo because she's "too old." Every human being has beauty at every age. Your challenge and responsibility is to help them relax enough to let it shine through.

Get creative with couples Instead of the standard posed portrait for the fiftieth wedding anniversary, try putting the couple in a familiar and comfortable environment and letting them interact with each other.

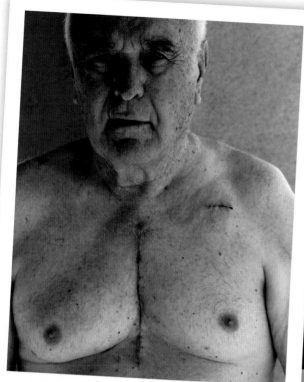

SHOW THE
Emotion

Think of meaningful feelings and concepts you'd like to illustrate with your photo: strength, perseverance, love, timeless, classic, heritage, contentment, outrageous.

SHOTS TO TRY:

Grandpa's chair ✱ Hands holding precious mementos ✱ Grandma's garden ✱ Grandma holding up her wedding dress ✱ Family resemblances even generations apart ✱ Re-create a photo from the past ✱ The family home, ranch or cabin ✱ Juxtaposing old and young (the texture of skin, hair and eyes) ✱ Storytelling ✱ Rocking chair ✱ Old apron ✱ Collections (war medals, books, etc.)

Andy Smylie

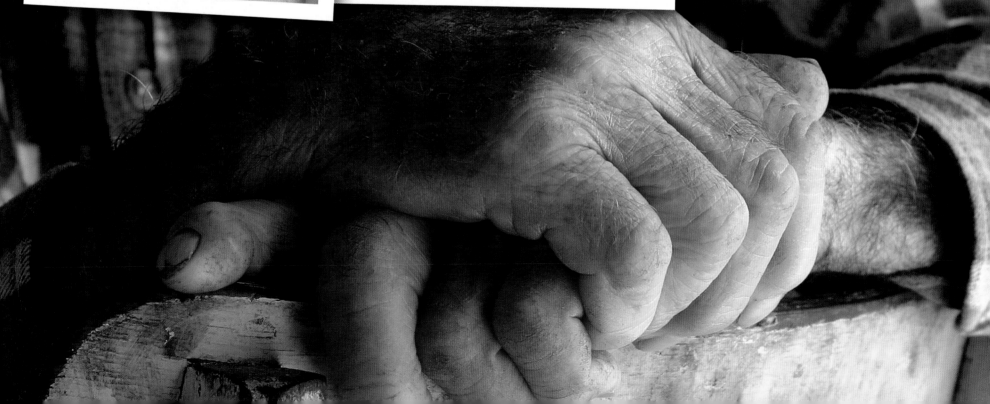

PHOTO ART
Show Off Your Family

After spending two months crowded into a van touring Europe, this family brought home some amazing memories and stacks and stacks of great photos. With no time to scrapbook but still wanting a tangible memory of the time together, this mother decided to make a photo collage and frame it in an old barn window that reminded her of the many villages they visited in their travels.

Donna Smylie

STEP-BY-STEP

① Find or purchase an old window frame with or without glass.

② Have photos printed primarily in 4" x 6" (10cm x 15cm) with a few 5" x 7" (13cm x 18cm) prints for variety.

③ Take a measurement from the inside of the window.

④ Cut matboard or foamcore to fit the inside dimensions.

⑤ Lay the matboard on a large table or the floor and play with the placement of the photos you are using.

⑥ Once you have a pleasing layout, use archival tape adhesive to secure the photos.

⑦ Once all the photos are placed, insert the photo-covered mat board into the window frame and secure by pounding small finish nails at a slight angle to the board. Note: If you are using a frame with glass, make sure to thoroughly clean the glass before you insert the photos.

Variations

✯ Place one huge photo over a background of smaller photos.

✯ In addition to photos, use brochures, matchbooks and other ephemera from your trip.

About the Authors

DONNA SMYLIE ❯ *Donna is a photographer who splits her time between Lakeland, Florida, and Mesa, Arizona. Originally from Australia, she is married to an Irishman with whom she has seven children and three amazingly gorgeous grandchildren. Co-owner of the former world-famous scrapbook store Memory Lane Photo and Paper Arts and co-author of* Designing with Photos, *she and her husband are the originators of the insanely popular 7gypsies line of the coolest products in the scrapbooking and paper arts world.*

ALLISON JONES ❯ *Allison is a photographer located in Mesa, Arizona. Married, with two children and five stepchildren, she is the co-owner of the former Memory Lane Photo and Paper Arts and co-author of the wildly successful photography book* Designing with Photos. *She is the former creative director for Autumn Leaves' Designing With book series and, on occasion, she designs products for 7gypsies. After retiring from retail in 2005, Allison launched Allison Tyler Jones Photography. Her studio work can be seen at www.atjphoto.com.*

About the Contributing Photographers

BARB UIL ❯ *Barb is a photographer from Canberra, Australia. First famous for her photo blog at www.blog.jinkyart.com.au, Barb's work has been published by* Shutterbug *and* Family Circle *magazines. Her style has been described as having "childhood cheekiness, editorial flair and narrative vision." She is married with two daughters. Her work can be seen at www.jinkyart.com.au.*

AUDREY WOULARD ❯ *Audrey is one of the most sought-after photographers in Chicago, Illinois. In addition to shooting portraits of chil-dren and their families, she also shoots model portfolios for Ford Modeling Agency's teen division. Her work has been published in magazines such as* InStyle *and* Better Homes and Gardens. *She uses only available light with her subjects. View more of her work at www.alwphotography.com.*

KATHRYN LANGFORD ❯ *Kathryn is a photographer located in Vancouver, British Columbia, Canada. She initially pursued a career in social work and is now a self-taught artist and entrepreneur. She recently expanded her portrait studio, which is dedicated to photographing children and pregnant mothers. Kathryn photographs exclusively in black-and-white film. View more of her work at www.photosby kathryn.com.*

AMANDA KEEYS ❯ *Amanda is a photographer located in Sydney, Australia. She is married with three kids (with another on the way) and has one dog and one cat. Her photos have been used as album-cover art for several international bands, and she has worked with the U.S. labels Focoloco and Go Goose Go. To view her personal photography projects, visit www.fallintoblue.com. Visit her commercial portrait Web site at www.amandakeeysphotography.com.*

JANELLE SMITH ❯ *Janelle is a photographer currently residing in Salt Lake City, Utah, with her husband, Zach, their sons, Zander and Ozzie, and their daughter, Zakrie. When not playing with her kids and many nephews, she enjoys reading, teaching classes and, of course, taking photos. Janelle has a Fine Arts Degree in Photography from Utah State University, and her work has been published in* Designing with Photos.

Special Thanks to the Following Photographers Who Also Contributed Their Images

- Kim Heffington
  www.kimheffington.com
- Ruth Giauque
- Andy Smylie
  www.andysmylie.com
- Austin Smylie
- Aliza Smylie

Favorite Web Sites

www.ittybittyactions.com
Plug-ins and Actions for Photoshop and Photoshop Elements, plus Barb Uil's famous Storyboard Actions to enhance your photos

www.atncentral.com
Tons of free Photoshop Actions

www.betterphoto.com
Short lessons on taking better photos

www.ilovephotography.com
A site dedicated to child portrait photographers

Albums/Embellishments/Papers

www.7gypsies.com
1-877-7GYPSY7 (749-7797)
The album and all the fun page tabs and embellishments used in the kids display project on pages 98–99 are from 7gypsies line of products.

www.kolousa.com
We have always loved Kolo albums for their simplicity and timeless style.

Further Reading on Photography

Understanding Exposure (Amphoto Books)
by Bryan Peterson
Probably the best, easiest-to-understand book about how to use your camera to get perfect exposure every time. A classic.

Designing with Photos (Autumn Leaves)
by Allison Tyler Jones and Donna Smylie
Our first photography book together and a forerunner to this book. The first half of the book is dedicated to photography and the second half to interesting projects using your photos.

Quote, Unquote: Volume 1 (Autumn Leaves, Creativity Inc.) compiled by Allison Tyler Jones
A wealth of quotes compiled in the cutest book. Perfect for all your memory projects. Many of the quotes in the gallery portion of this book were taken from *Quote, Unquote*.

The Photoshop CS2 Book for Digital Photographers (New Riders Press)
by Scott Kelby
If you are going to buy one book on Photoshop, make sure it's by Scott Kelby. He's a guru but he explains everything in plain old English.